AF574667

The Book of Origins

General editor: Pinin Carpi
Educational co-ordinator: Ivana Bonissone
Editors: Giovanni Baccini, Claudia Zavatarelli
Editor of English text: Alison Sage
Educational advisers: Robert King, Philip Claris
Adviser on Natural Science: Ettore Tibaldi, from the Zoology department of the University of Milan
Contributors: Ermanno Libenzi, Luigi Marcon
Original drawings: Gabriele Amadori, Valentina Carpi, Paolo Giorsetti, Desideria Guicciardini, Colin McNaughton, Valentino Parmiani, Gianni Pegoraro, Michele Sambin
Design: Liliana Biroldi, Emme Edizioni and DP Press Ltd, Sevenoaks, Kent
Photographic research: Marco Bellavita, Livia Sismondi
Things to do devised by Luciano Biolcati and Maria Mari
Typeset in England by Type Practitioners Limited, Sevenoaks, Kent
Printed in Italy by Istituto Geografico de Agostini, Novara
First published in the English language by
Ernest Benn Limited, 1980
25 New Street Square, London EC4A 3JA
& Sovereign Way, Tonbridge, Kent TN9 1RW

ISBN 0 510-00073-8

The Book of

Origins

Ernest Benn Limited
London & Tonbridge

About this book

How did the world begin? What were the first animals? How did they live?

This book explores these questions, explaining some of the latest theories and matching them with the very oldest accounts of the birth of the world. It shows why we believe we began as tiny micro-organisms and how we came to discover more about ourselves and our surroundings.

There are photographs of living fossils: plants and animals which have hardly changed over millions of years and are present-day clues to our distant past. Starting from life today, this book takes a journey back in time to show how human beings developed frcm apeman to wandering hunter, from hunter to settled farmer. Further back still, when our ancestors were no bigger than a shrew, lived the huge dinosaurs. Why did they disappear, after ruling the earth for more than 150 million years? Today, we may have the answer; although the jigsaw puzzle of prehistory still has many vital pieces missing. Earlier still, you can see the creatures who lived before the dinosaurs and how we believe the very first forms of life emerged from primeval seas.

What will happen to us next? It is hard to guess; but certainly it will help us shape our future if we understand some of the things that have made us what we are.

Contents

The time travellers

It all began on a hot afternoon at the beginning of the summer holidays. Sam (that's my brother) and I were in the garden feeling a bit bored. I could see Mum through the window, painting the kitchen walls, and Dad was trying to fix some tiles around the sink. He was getting annoyed because he hates do-it-yourself. Suddenly, he saw us. "Sam!" he yelled. "Charlotte! It's about time you two tidied up your things for a change. How many times have I told you that I can't get at my tool box with that heap of rubbish of yours in the way?"

A few weeks ago, Mum had bought a couple of boxes of old toys and things at a jumble sale and put them in the garage. Now, all of a sudden, it was *our* fault. I know we wouldn't let Dad throw any of it away, but still, it wasn't fair of him to go on about it.

Anyway, Sam and I ended up going into the garage. It was quite interesting really, once we started poking about in all that old junk. "Let's take some of it out on the lawn," said Sam. "It's too dark to see properly in here." So we did.

There was an old bath with claw feet, lots of broken bits of toy cars and things, a couple of old brooms, a bicycle dynamo, some funny metal pots and pans and, best of all, a beautiful old alarm clock. It was made of a strange brassy kind of metal with a wonderful bell on the top and it had the loveliest ivory hands, pointing to twelve o'clock. I liked it a lot; but Sam said he wanted it because he had to get up earlier than I did to go to school. I said I needed it just as much as he did, and we argued. In the end, I grabbed at it.

Suddenly, the alarm started ringing loudly and it made us both jump. Then, while we stared at it, a shiny, smooth black string snaked out from under the bell. "Weird," said Sam. "It's like something out of a science-fiction book," I said. "It must be a really special kind of clock."

We looked at it a bit carefully, in case it was a bomb. Then I said something about time machines, and I'm not sure whose idea it was actually, - maybe it was Sam's, he always said it was his - we decided to build a time machine.

It didn't take very long with all that junk around and we quite enjoyed it. Sam always fancies himself a bit of an engineer and he did some clever things with the bits of cars for an engine. I'm more of an inventor. I thought of things like a life-support system with the old pots and an amazing radio transmitter which carried thoughts, not sounds. "Because sounds are too slow," I explained to Sam.

Then we came to the clock. "This is going to be what starts the machine," said Sam, firmly. "So I'm fixing the string to the engine." It seemed a very good idea.

"Let's do a test run," I suggested. "We could use one of the old dolls as a dummy person." We stuffed an old, wooden doll with fluffy blond hair into the pilot's seat. Then, very importantly, Sam started tugging on the string.

"No; I've a better idea," I said. "Let's turn the clock back. That's the best way of starting a time machine." So he did.

Suddenly, the alarm rang out again. There was a sort of flurry in the air, as though a car had just gone past - and the machine vanished. Just like that. Sam and I stood there, staring, not saying a word. We both thought we were seeing things; or rather, not seeing things.

"It's *gone*!" said Sam, softly.

"I know," I said. "But you've still got the clock." And so he had. It said half past four.

"Maybe, if we turn it *forward* again, to where it was, everything will come back," he suggested.

"Good idea," I said.

Shaking a bit, he pushed the winder forward until the hands said twelve. Again, there was a slight breeze, as if something had fluttered its wings - and there was our time machine, sitting on the lawn again. But there was nothing in it. The doll had gone.

"Let's do it again," said Sam. "Maybe we will get the doll back."

"Wait!" I yelled. "Selina's in the machine!" Our black kitten, Selina, had just disappeared over the edge of the bath, tail waving. But it was too late. Sam had already moved the hands and the alarm

was ringing. The machine vanished again. "Bring her back," I said. "Quick, or she'll disappear, like the doll."

Sam moved back the winder; and the machine reappeared. But there was no cat. Mikko, our white dog, came padding up to see what was going on. He whined miserably and sniffed the grass. He liked Selina.

"What shall we do?" I whispered. "We *must* get Selina back."

"We'll send Mikko after her," said Sam, and we put Mikko in the machine.

"Where *is* she?" I asked.

"What do you mean?" said Sam.

"Well," I said, "what time did you send Selina back to?"

"I can't remember," said Sam going pale. "You started shouting at me and so I turned the hands back straight away." But he must still have been fiddling with the winder, because the alarm suddenly rang. The machine vanished; and when it reappeared, Mikko had gone.

"*We'll* have to go back now," I said, not feeling at all brave.

"All right," said Sam. "Just a little way at first." I don't know what he really felt about it, but I wasn't at all sure that I wanted to leave our nice green lawn with the daisies in it.

He turned back the hands of the clock just a fraction. The alarm rang and suddenly the sky went dark, like it does if you're just going to faint. I felt as if I was tumbling through space and I could hardly breathe. Everything stopped. And there we were, in a field of poppies. It was odd, but I knew that field. So did Sam.

"It's France," he said, firmly.

"Yes," I said, "it's just like that place we went on holiday last year. Do you remember?"

"If it *is*," he said, "there should be some caves near here, with funny paintings in them. You know, the ones that were supposed to be made by cave men."

I nodded. I did remember. Carefully, we climbed out of the machine. I stamped hard on the grass, to see if I was real and solid and not a ghost. But the grass flattened, just as it would have done in our garden, and I felt much better. "Hold on to that clock," I said. The thought of losing it was too awful even to think about. Sam just nodded.

Without a word, we walked across the field. It was a hot, still day and I could hear the larks high up in the sky, singing fit to burst. Grasshoppers chirped and little dry creatures rustled in the long grass. At the edge of the field were some rocks and they led, as we knew from last year, to the entrance

to the rabbit warren of caves.

It was cool and dark in the caves and we couldn't see a thing at first, I had a packet of mints in my pocket and we sat down and sucked one. Suddenly, I heard voices; and I *knew* who was coming. It was the oddest, strangest, horridest feeling I have ever had. Round a corner of the rocks came a boy and a girl with a dog - and they were us! It was me and Sam and Mikko - only one year younger!

I looked at Sam and he knew what I was thinking. "Let's go," he whispered, and we crept out of the cave without being seen. We walked back to the machine in silence. "That was us!" said Sam, at last.

"Who are we, then?" I said. "We can't be two people at once."

Sam thought hard. "We must be in two different time planes," he said.

Most times, I would have laughed at him and told him that he was talking rubbish, but now I really wanted someone to understand what was going on. So I kept quiet. Then I said, "Shall we go on backwards? I want to find Mikko." I really wanted to see him. He belonged to everything normal and in the right time and place.

"I think it was about eleven o'clock." said Sam, turning the winder. Blurry stars flashed past my face and my stomach seemed to turn inside out. Then everything stopped whirling and we were sitting on the edge of a huge forest of pine trees.

"Where are we?" I whispered.

"Don't know," said Sam, "but it must be before we were born." When he said that, I had a nasty feeling inside. I thought about all the ages and all the thousands of people who had come and gone before me and Sam and Mikko and Selina. Even before Mum and Dad. Suddenly I saw that I didn't know anything about any of them. "Maybe," I said slowly, "maybe we have gone back to the time when those cave paintings were being made."

Just at that moment, a tall boy dressed in what looked like a rough leather tunic, came dashing through the clearing in front of us. He had thick black hair and he was about the same age as Sam. He was being chased by a girl with dark hair, shrieking with laughter - and a white dog: Mikko!

But this is only the beginning of the story. I'll tell you more about it later; how we found Selina, too, and even the boring old doll, which had gone to a time before people even existed. When we got back, Dad was really mad about all the junk on the lawn and he made us clear up everything. It's odd to think that he and Mum never knew how far we travelled that day, or how nearly we never came home.

The past in the present

1 All over the world, people have *initiation* ceremonies, when children become adults in the eyes of the rest of their society. In the West, we have them too, although perhaps they are not so obvious. Here, some Papuan boys are being accepted as men in their tribe in New Guinea.

2 This tribesman has a stone, carefully shaped to fit a wooden shaft to make a club. This is for ceremonial use, as you can see from the decoration.

3 Early hunters and farmers, like these Papuans, often had to travel long distances to find food.

In the beginning

In the beginning, there were no pens, pencils or paper. There were no books and no-one could read or write. This is the time we call prehistory because there are no written records to describe the daily life or even the great events of these early people who lived before writing had been invented. But they did leave all kinds of clues. They left their tools, their ornaments, and sometimes even games and traces of their villages and towns. In this way we can make a good guess about the way these people lived, although there are many gaps in our knowledge.

Some of the best clues to the past, however, lie in the present. There are still today in some parts of the world tribes who live just as they have done for thousands of years. Through them, we can see how our own ancestors may have lived.

Papua-New Guinea is one of the richest areas of primitive art, ritual and tradition. Here, until quite recently, the tribes in the interior have been allowed to live almost undisturbed, and their way of life is as highly organized as any modern society, although they still use stone-age tools.

4 These are Papuan arrow heads carved from bone.

5 A Papuan ritual dance called a *Sing Sing*. ▶

1 These boys belong to the El Molo tribe in East Africa. At dawn, they go to the lake to fish.

2 When the fish are caught, they are cleaned straight away. This woman is going to make a meal.

3 Meanwhile, a boy is breaking up wood with a stone to make a fire so that his sister can cook.

4 The youngest children have a small hut all to themselves.

Where the stone age is still alive

The El Molo people who live on the shores of Lake Rudolph (now called Lake Turkana) in Kenya, still live rather like early man. We call them hunter-gatherers because that is how they get their food - partly by catching fish and partly by collecting roots and vegetables. They live in small huts made of straw and cloth and they have very few possessions. Their wealth lies in their knowledge of how to survive in their surroundings - how to catch fish, where to find food plants and how to live together in the safest, most friendly fashion.

They live in groups of about twenty, although the whole tribe numbers about five hundred. Each group likes visiting the others, however, as many of them are closely related by marriage, and the El Molo feel that family ties are very important.

Their boats are made of tree trunks, tied together with tough grasses to make a kind of raft, and they mostly spear their fish with harpoons, rather like a hunter spears an animal on land.

5 The older children take turns at harpoon practice. Here, they are trying to throw the harpoon through a ring tossed into the air.

6 Now his skill is being put to the test. This boy is going off alone to fish with his harpoon.

1 These houses on stilts, called *pile-dwellings* are in the Pacific islands of New Hebrides. We believe that early man sometimes built similar houses on water.

2,3 These boys are preparing for their own initiation ceremony which will prove that they can take their part as adults with the tribe.

Initiation ceremonies

All over the world, people hold a ceremony which they think of as a *second* birth. It shows that a child has become an adult. We call it an *initiation* ceremony and it marks the beginning of a child's new life as a full member of his society. In the West, too, we hold a kind of initiation ceremony; if someone wants to join a club or group, they may have to pass a test to show the other members that they are able to take part.

When boys from a tribe in New Guinea reach a certain age, they are taken into the forest and left to make their own way back to the village. When they finally return home, there is a big feast to celebrate and from then onwards they are treated as adults. Of course, from the moment they could walk, they had been learning to live in the forest and so this ceremony is rather like a test to see if they can put to use all they know. Not all initiation ceremonies are as dangerous as this one. Sometimes, children simply have to go to a place apart from the rest of the tribe, where they are taught all about the special laws of their tribe. These ceremonies are usually very private, and no-one (except those taking part) is allowed to see or hear what takes place.

4 A tower of wood is built in the forest as the first part of the ceremony.

5 Now the boys must leap off the top of the tower, and their only protection is a rope tied to their ankles. It takes a lot of courage to jump! ▶

Jasper - or how the wolf was outwitted

Once, many years ago, there lived a poor widow. She had thirteen sons, but the cleverest of them all was Jasper, the youngest. He was as small as a gnat; but what he lacked in size he made up in cunning.

One day, the old woman called all her sons together. "Listen," she said, "I am old, and I have taught you all I can. It is time for you to go out into the world and find your own fortunes. Go, now, with my blessing."

"Let us go to the King," said the eldest. "He is sure to need servants." The others agreed, and after a few days' travel they arrived at the castle, tired and hungry. They knocked so loudly on the gate that the King himself asked to see the strangers.

"Your Majesty," said the eldest brother, "we have come here to be your servants. But first we beg you for a bed for the night and some food."

"I have no need of beggars," said the King, "but I will take you in on one condition: that you bring back the bedcover which belongs to the Wild Wolf in the forest." And he laughed.

The brothers said nothing; no-one had yet stepped inside the Wild Wolf's lair and lived to tell the story. Then little Jasper spoke up. "My Lord, if you will give me a long, sharp needle, I will bring you the bedcover." And that same evening he set off alone into the forest.

Soon he found the Wolf's lair and he climbed up onto the roof, slid down the chimney and tiptoed into the bedroom. The Wolf had not yet returned, so Jasper crawled under the bed to wait.

When night fell, the Wolf came home and threw himself down on his bed to sleep. Out crept Jasper and began poking the Wolf with his long needle.

"Itch and scratch, itch and scratch,
My bed is like a bramble patch." grumbled the Wolf sleepily, and he tossed and turned so much that the bedcover fell off. Straight away, Jasper snatched it up and ran back to the King.

Now the Wolf had a parrot who could tell the time like a clock and answer any question in the world. In the morning, the Wolf woke early, feeling cold.

"Parrot, what time is it?" he asked.

"Six o'clock," said the parrot, fixing him with a beady black eye, "and Jasper has stolen your bed-cover."

"Jasper!" shouted the Wolf. "Who is this Jasper?"

"Jasper is a thirteenth son, as small as a gnat but as cunning as an old fox," answered the parrot.

"Then I shall roast him alive if I see him," said the Wolf.

Meanwhile, the greedy King had had an idea. "Jasper," he said, "you have done well. But if you will fetch the Wolf's pillow, which is covered with little bells, I will give you and your family so much gold that they will never be in need again."

Jasper saw that he had no choice, and he bowed

low, "As you wish, My Lord. But can I please have some clay?"

This was brought to him immediately, and soon Jasper was on his way to the Wolf's lair. Just as before, he hid under the bed to wait for night.

As soon as the Wolf was sound asleep, Jasper crawled out of his hiding-place and began stuffing the bells with clay, so that they would not ring. Then, as soft as thistledown, he slipped the pillow from under the Wolf's head.

The Wolf woke early with a stiff neck. "Parrot, what time is it?" he shouted sleepily.

"Five o'clock," said the parrot, "and Jasper has stolen your pillow."

"My pillow!" shouted the Wolf. "I'll grind his bones to powder, if ever I catch him!"

In his castle, the King was plotting. Could he kill Jasper and keep his gold? "Jasper," he said angrily, "you are a master thief and you deserve to die. But if you will capture the Wolf, I will pardon you and reward your family richly."

What could poor Jasper do? "I've no chance either way," he thought sadly, but he said, "My Lord, if you will give me a cart, a horse and a wooden box, I will do my best."

A few hours later, he was driving the cart towards the Wolf's lair where he met the Wolf himself. Hiding his fright as best he could, Jasper began singing a little song:

"Jasper is dead, bury him deep.
He lost his head and no-one will weep."

"What's that you're singing?" said the Wolf.

"That wicked thief, Jasper," said Jasper, "he's been caught at last and the King has chopped his head off."

The Wolf showed his teeth, "I wanted to kill him myself," he said.

"Never mind," said Jasper. "Why don't you help me with his coffin? He was about the same size as you are so perhaps you could try it for size."

"Gladly," said the Wolf, and leapt into the box. Quick as a flash, Jasper nailed down the lid.

"What are you doing, boy?" shouted the Wolf. "Let me out this minute!"

"I'm taking you to the King," said Jasper calmly. "So stop your shouting and find some manners." And he set the box on his cart, took the magic parrot and a bag of gold from the Wolf's lair and set off for the King's castle.

But this time he did not go straight to the King. He left the Wolf-box at the gate and went to fetch his brothers; because although he was as small as a gnat, he was a cunning as an old fox, and he did not trust the King one centimetre.

Quietly, before dawn, they all slipped away back to their cottage. For with the magic parrot and the bag of gold, they could settle down happily for the rest of their lives.

1 Children learn faster than adults and (like this African boy) they begin to learn from their parents.

3 This little Chinese baby is learning all the time on his mother's back. She is giving him what we call a 'cultural heritage'; she is teaching him about the world before he was born so that he will be able to understand his surroundings.

2 This is Kenya, in East Africa. This baby elephant has not yet learned to find food for himself and so he is suckled by his mother.
▼

When we begin to learn

When did the world begin for you? It only began from the day you were born. If you want to know what happened before then, you must ask someone older, or look in a book. Humans have one very big advantage over other animals: they can pass on information to their children and to their children's children.

If you think of the history of the world as being a book 1000 pages long, recognisable human beings only arrived somewhere

4 This little baboon is also learning about the world from his mother. Like humans, baboons have a longer childhood than other animals.

5 In many species, the males help to look after their children. Here, a male grey partridge is sitting on the eggs.

6 Among humans, men often spend a lot of time with their children, playing with them and looking after them. This aborigine is taking his baby son for a walk.

around the second half of the last page. Biologically speaking, this is very recent indeed and not long enough for us to have developed our minds very much. So why are we living so differently from our ancestors? Largely because each new baby can learn from all the thousands of things that have happened before he was born. We call this our 'cultural heritage', because it was shaped in part by many generations before our own.

8 This boy, too, has learned to climb. The more you experiment, the more you find out. That is how humans learn about the world they live in.

7 This Indian monkey has learned how to climb. Now, for the first time, he can reach the tops of the trees.

1 Often, parents teach their children without even knowing what they are doing. They teach them to talk, to walk, to laugh and to use their hands. Here an African father is being watched with great interest by his baby son, as he digs for insects with a sharp stick.

2 This Somalian father is teaching his son how to use a bow and arrow.

3 Here the father shows his son the best way to hold the bow.

4 And here, the boy is trying it out for himself.

Lessons without schools

From the moment you were born, you began to learn. Humans are born with very little unlearned (or *instinctive*) knowledge. Because they need to do so much finding out, they grow up more slowly than any other animal. Did you know that in the first three years of your life, you learned faster than at any other time? This is because children learn much more easily than grown-ups. This doesn't only mean the kind of learning you do in school. It means learning how to talk and make friends, deciding what you like and exploring your surroundings.

It seems very likely that one of the reasons why early man developed his mind was that he lived in a group where he *had* to be aware of what was happening around him. In addition, every new thing he learnt from others helped him to learn something more.

Amongst many tribes, the children do not go to school as you do. But they still have to learn about their surroundings in just the same way. They learn how to hunt and fish; how to track an animal silently and which roots and berries are good to eat. They learn in the best possible way: by watching, and then trying to do things for themselves. They don't exactly have examinations, but only skill will mean that the long and patient hours spent stalking an animal will be rewarded with success.

5 This is a Masai village in Kenya. A father is explaining to his son how to hunt with a spear.

6 The spear must be held firmly, but gently, to make the throw easier and more accurate.

7 One day, this boy will be a hunter himself, and he will show *his* son how to use a spear.

1 These ferns which carpet the woods are very similar to the ones that grew on the earth long before man appeared. By looking at primitive plants such as these we can try to work out what life was like on this planet many millions of years ago.

2 This is an iguana from the Galapagos Islands. Many very strange primitive creatures live here because it has been cut off from the rest of the world for thousands of years.

3 These Komodo dragons which come from South East Asia probably look something like the dinosaurs of pre-history.

Living fossils

The tribes on the previous pages can give us some idea of how early man lived thousands of years ago. It can only give us a rough impression, of course, because their lives have changed a little over the centuries. But they have not altered as much as we have. Why? In many cases they have not needed, or been made, to change. When an animal fits comfortably into its surroundings, naturally enough, it stays very much as it is. For this reason, you can still find many primitive creatures, who are the direct descendants of animals which lived long before man ever stood on two feet.

And it is not only true of animals, but plants too. Occasionally in coal (which perhaps you knew was fossilized plants) you can see the imprint of beautiful ferns from many millions of years ago which do not look so different from our own today. Coniferous trees, like pines or firs, existed before the world had ever seen a flowering plant, and yet descendants of these trees are still found everywhere.

4 This is not a hedgehog. It is a spiny anteater, one of the most primitive animals still living. It lays eggs and is very distantly related to the first mammals of all.

5 This duck billed platypus comes from Australia. It is a mammal, although it too, lays eggs.

Signs of our past

1 This statue was discovered on the island of Cyprus. It is *neolithic* – the age when man had learned to polish stone. It shows that even at this distant date, man wanted to express himself. He was not only interested in food and shelter.

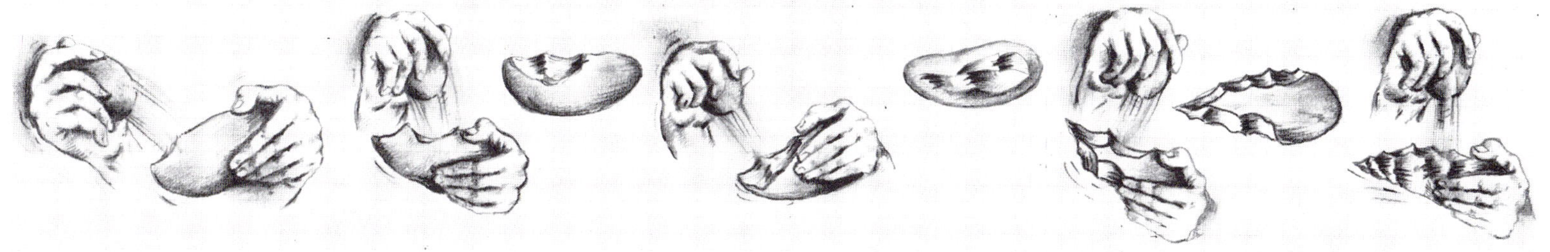

2 Here you can see how a flint tool was made. One stone is used to chip off little flakes from another, to make a sharp point and a cutting edge.

The first tools

When did man first begin to use tools? Some people think that it was about the time he began walking on two legs, as this left his hands free for holding things. Probably, this was when he began to take the important step of leaving the protection of the thick forest for the more open grasslands. He was in more danger, but he had more opportunity for learning and discovery.

Before long, he had learned to make use of his *precision grip*. Touch your forefinger with your thumb. No other animal can do this so accurately, and it is the reason why humans can hold a needle or steer an ocean liner; throw a beachball or make a complicated piece of machinery.

First of all, early man simply picked up loose stones. Then he found that one stone could be chipped with another to make a sharp, cutting edge. This was a tremendous discovery; now he could make a whole range of tools. He began exchanging tools with other men; he began exploring further and further. We believe that, from his original home in Africa, the ancestor of modern man now began to colonize Europe and Asia, and even America.

By this time, man had begun to create things for pleasure as well as for survival, for all kinds of beautiful flint shapes, far too fine to be of practical use, have been found. In the Shanidar Cave in Iraq, we have discovered a grave, 60,000 years old, and to the archaeologists' surprise, the dead man had been covered with flowers. Early man must have thought about his friends and family. His life was not just one long struggle for survival. He had begun a culture for himself.

3 These flint tools came from the *paleolithic* age, the time when man first began chipping one flint with another.

4 This is a smooth stone axe from the New Stone (*neolithic*) Age. By this time, man was grinding stone and bone to make it smooth.

The cave of mysteries

I promised to tell you about our holiday in France, the summer before we built our time machine.

One afternoon, we begged a candle off Jeanette, the caretaker, because the day before, Sam had seen a dark crack in the rocks near the village and we guessed it might be a cave.

We set off across the fields with Mikko, our dog. It was so hot that everything seemed to shake in the haze. The earth smelled powdery dry and the corn stalks crackled underfoot. When we reached the rocks, we could see there *was* a cave.

"Come on, then," said Sam. But he didn't move. "All right," I said. "Let's light the candle."

It smelled musty in the cave and I was cold and shivery after the heat outside. "I bet no-one's been here for years," said Sam, going on ahead.

"Wait," I said, "I can't see! And what if there are lots of passages? We'll get lost."

"I've thought of that," he said proudly, and he took some chalk out of his pocket. "We'll make marks on the walls and then we can follow them back." He looked at me. "Are you scared?"

"No," I said, untruthfully. "But I've got this funny feeling." I couldn't really explain but I'd felt that something was odd all afternoon.

"Let's hold hands. I'd feel better if we did." Sam's very good like that. He doesn't mind saying he's scared.

We went on for a bit until the passage widened. Sam held up the candle - and almost dropped it. There, on the wall, were the most amazing pictures I have ever seen. There were hundreds of animals, leaping and running, and little stick men, chasing them with spears. "Who could have done them?" said Sam.

Just then, Mikko howled and ran off into the darkness. "Mikko!" I shouted. "Come here!"

Suddenly, we panicked, Sam and I, and we ran too, not even bothering to look at the chalk marks. We didn't stop until we were outside in the sunshine. Mikko was still whining and running round in circles. It took him ages to calm down and then we didn't feel like going back into the cave.

Next time we did, Dad came too (in the end, we had told him and Mum) and he said that we had discovered something really exciting. We had found some cave paintings done by Stone Age people, thousands of years ago.

Then all kinds of experts and professors and journalists came and had a look. We were quite famous and had our pictures in the local paper, although they spelt my name wrong and said Sam was ten and he's eleven, which annoyed him a bit.

One strange thing happened which I never told anyone. When we went back to the cave with Dad, I found a packet of mints, the kind I always buy. And they were in a new kind of wrapping – which I didn't see in the shops until *months* after we found the cave....

1 In this dry valley in Tierra del Fuego (The Land of Fire) in South America there are caves where early man once lived.

2 This is the entrance to the cave, now called the Cave of Hands.

3 Tierra del Fuego is ▶ in the far south of Chile. Here it is mostly desert today, but thousands of years ago it was much wetter.

Early man was an artist

About 30,000 years ago, man had begun to make pictures - maybe even earlier.

Over 100 years ago, an archaeologist was exploring some caves in Spain with his nine-year-old daughter, when he heard her shouting excitedly, "Look! Look at these pictures of bulls!" She had found the beautiful prehistoric paintings at Altamira. Strangely enough, none of the experts of the time would believe that such fine work could be so old. "It's a forgery," they said. And they went on saying this until so much evidence mounted up that they *had* to believe that all those thousands of years ago, man was a brilliant artist.

What did he paint? He painted the animals around him like elk and buffalo, mammoth and rhinoceros. With great detail he drew running deer and horses and even a donkey! Sometimes he even showed the muscles and bones of these animals under their skins.

Why did he paint? We can only guess. Perhaps because he liked doing it, or perhaps because it was a kind of magic to him. He may have painted a successful hunt to bring him good luck. He also

4 Only desert animals ▶ make their homes here, like this armadillo. (You will see him again on p 116.)

◀ **5** Hundreds of handprints on the walls of this cave are perhaps all that remain of some ancient initiation ceremony. Can you see that they are all *left* hand prints?

6 These mysterious signs are probably ancient magic symbols. Maybe we shall never understand their meaning. ▶

made hand prints, perhaps as a sign that he had been there and that it was *his* work.

On these pages, you can see a cave in the mountains of South America. It is such a hot, dry country that it is called Tierra del Fuego (The Land of Fire). Perhaps when our ancestors lived here, it was much wetter and there were many more trees and flowers. You can see hand prints made by men, women and children from thousands of years ago. You can also see some animals called *guanaco*, rather like llamas, which they hunted for food and for their skins.

7 Here is a herd of guanaco (a sort of llama) in flight. See how beautifully the artist has captured the movement with only a few lines.

1 This is the 'Cave of Cannibals' on Easter Island in the Pacific Ocean. The ceiling is painted with magic symbols.

Cave paintings

Why did early man paint in caves? We believe that he painted everywhere, but it is mainly the cave art which has survived. Deep in the rocks, his pictures, painted with coloured earth which is easily damaged, have been left undisturbed until recent times.

Strangely enough, although it is clear that early man could paint with incredible delicacy and movement, there are few realistic pictures of peoples' faces. Perhaps he felt it was dangerous or unlucky to make pictures of himself, except as a symbol. We have found many sign pictures. Maybe these are magic symbols: perhaps – and we still do not know – they were the very first form of writing.

2 This is the wall of a cave in Tanzania. You can see men and animals. Is the figure in the centre with the cloak a chief? And is the tiny figure a child?

3 This cave is in Australia. You can see someone fishing with a net.

4 These horses and an auroch (an early breed of cattle) were painted over 25,000 years ago on the walls of a cave at Lascaux, in France.

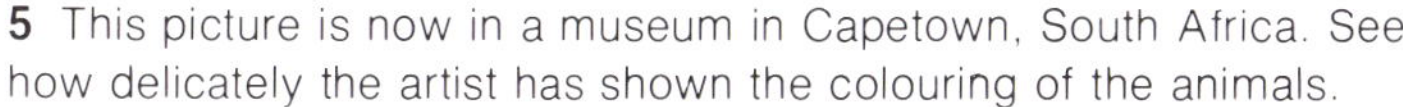

5 This picture is now in a museum in Capetown, South Africa. See how delicately the artist has shown the colouring of the animals.

6 This artist has brilliantly captured the movement of this herd of cattle. The painting was discovered in a cave in Algeria, North Africa.

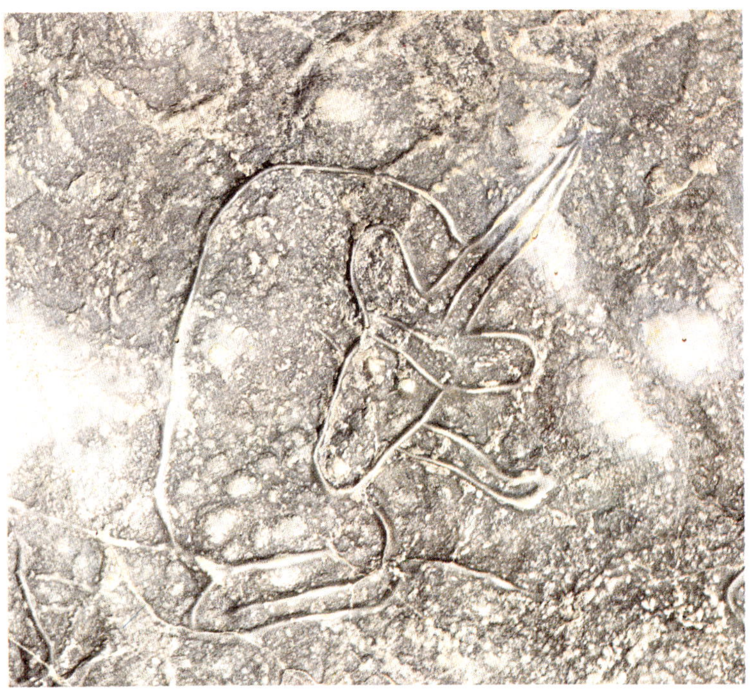

1 This deer is carved on the rock at the oasis of Iherir in Algeria. Is it sleeping, or perhaps licking itself?

2 These hunting scenes were carved on rocks in Valcamonica, Italy.

. . . and sculptures

Not only did early man draw and paint, he also made sculptures. Sometimes, he carved on the walls of his cave. Sometimes, he carved bone and stone into ornaments and little figures. His jewellery was often very beautiful - beads carved into tiny animals, or geometric designs, which were made to hang round the neck. Perhaps they were worn simply because they were pretty; but perhaps they were also used as *amulets*. An amulet is a charm to keep the wearer safe from harm.

These early artists were able to capture what was important in the things they carved in a way that modern artists can still envy and admire.

3 This mysterious face is probably a magic symbol. Notice how it appears deliberately to have no expression.

4 These aurochs, (a kind of cattle), were carved in an Algerian cave.

5 This carved bison's head was found at Saint Germain en Laye. It is at least 14,000 years old, but the sculptor was as skilled as any modern artist.

1 Near the Dead Sea is a rock called *Lot's Wife*. The Bible says that she disobeyed God by looking at the burning city of Sodom. As a punishment, she was turned into a pillar of salt. Of course, this particular rock is neither salt, nor is it a fossil; but we can still wonder what really happened. Perhaps she fell into one of the salt flats beside the Dead Sea!

How fossils are made

What is a fossil? Over thousands of years, minerals soak into the bones of dead creatures, slowly turning them to stone. It is strange to think that we can look at the bones of creatures that died millions of years ago.

How can we tell when they lived? By detective work. If we know the age of the rock where we find the fossil, we can date it. By looking at fossilized teeth, we can tell whether the creature ate other animals or whether it lived on plants. We can tell if it could fly or if it lived in the sea, by looking at the arm and leg bones. We even know that dinosaurs laid eggs because we have discovered some, turned to stone!

But scientists face one big difficulty. Fossils only survived in certain places: therefore, they can only find out about a fraction of the creatures which must have lived on the earth. But sometimes, they have a piece of luck; a mammoth (a huge hairy elephant which no longer exists) was discovered, perfectly preserved in the ice. Now, scientists could see exactly what the animal looked like. He even had the remains of his last meal in his stomach! But there are still many, many gaps in our knowledge, and so many clues waiting to be discovered.

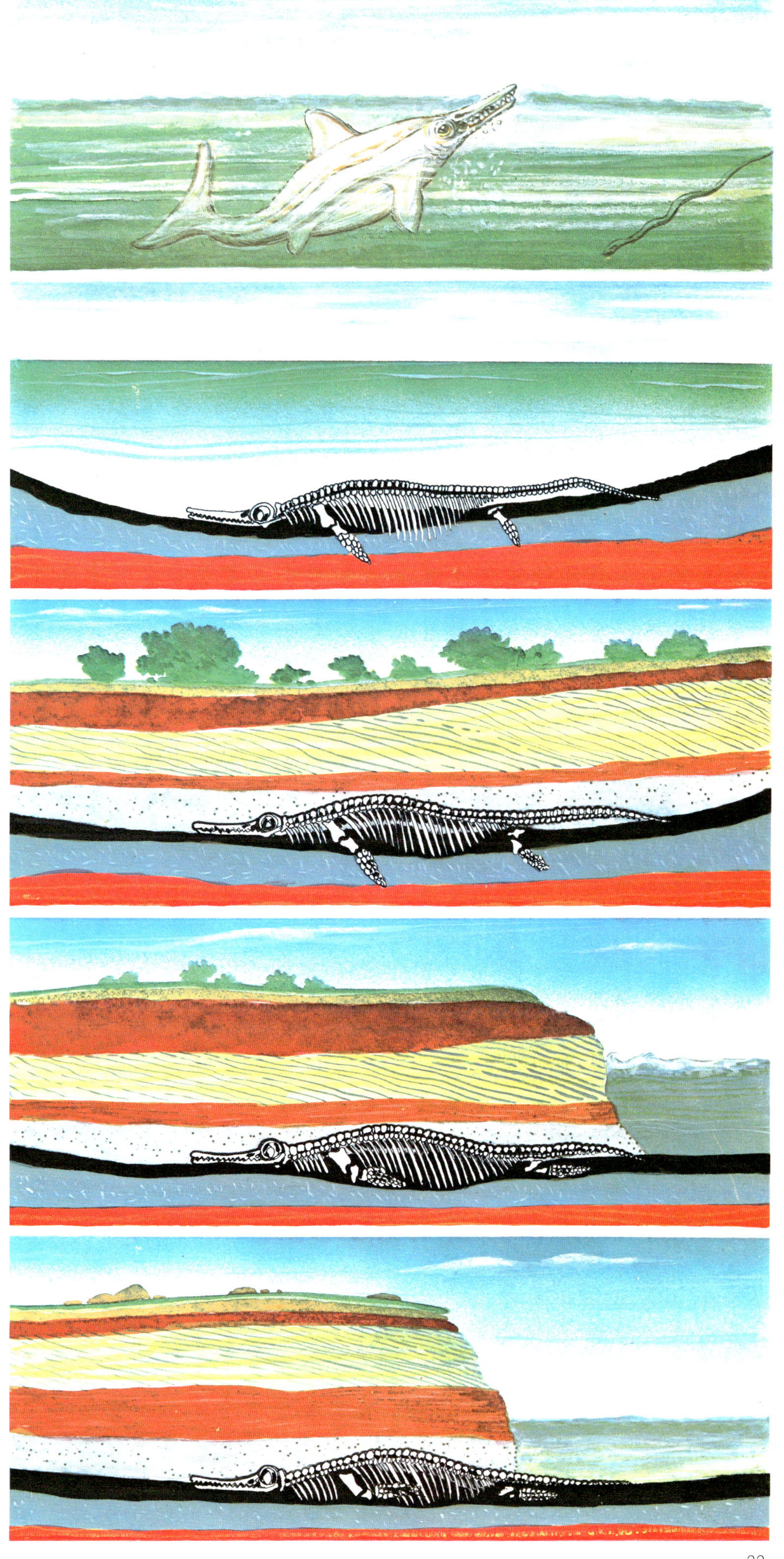

2 An *ichthyosaur* dies and its bones are covered with mud. In time, more layers press down on the mud, turning it to soft rock. The ichthyosaur begins to turn to stone. Then the sea wears away the rock and we see the fossilized bones on the shore. ▶

1 This is near Verona in Italy. The fossils can tell us the history of the earth, layer by layer.

2 Here, a fish, millions of years old, has been preserved in the stone.

3 This looks like a beautiful sculpture; it is the fossil of a marine creature.

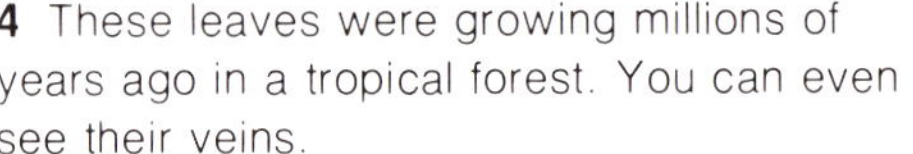

4 These leaves were growing millions of years ago in a tropical forest. You can even see their veins.

5 This is a fossil shellfish, called an *ammonite*. You can sometimes find them on the seashore.

Fossils

It is not only the skeletons of creatures which become fossils. Sometimes we find the impression of their skin and claws in the surrounding rock. We have even discovered dinosaurs' fossilized footprints and, from these, scientists think they can guess how fast they were able to run!

Sometimes, you can see a shining fern pattern on a lump of coal. This is because coal *is* fossilized trees, grasses and plants which, over millions of years, were squeezed flat until they turned

6 This is another kind of shellfish. It, too, was swimming in the sea millions of years ago.

7 Even prehistoric flies have been preserved in stone. Can you see the impression of its wings?

8 This insect is preserved in *amber* – the fossilized resin, or sap, of ancient trees.

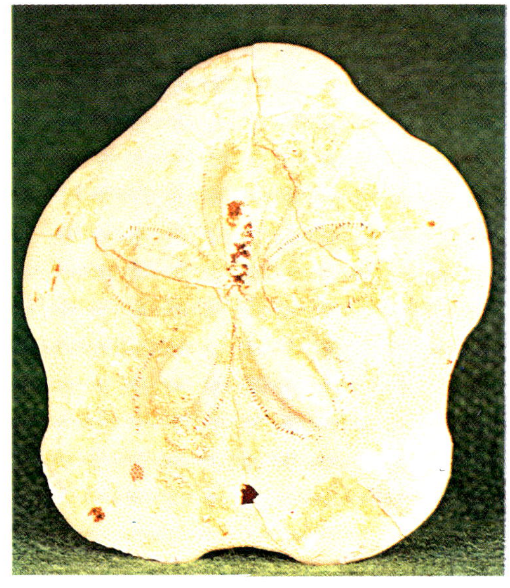

9 This sea urchin is a fossil too. The flower pattern is the impression made by its insides.

10 These are fossil leaves of a kind of early oak tree.

into concentrated fuel - coal. Oil, too is a *fossil fuel.* It is also formed from the remains of ancient forests.

From fossils, we know that most of England was once covered with tropical forests and swamps. Ancestors of our crocodile basked on the sandbanks, while turtles and great seabirds swam on the water. The very first horses, only about one metre high, galloped up and down beaches fringed with palm trees and circled by coral reefs.

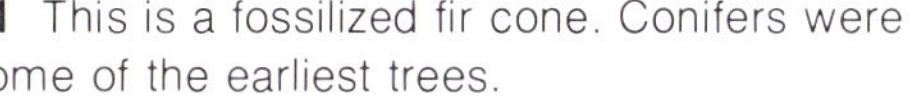

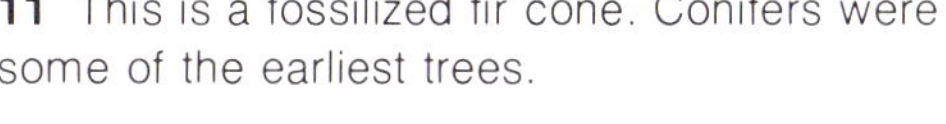

11 This is a fossilized fir cone. Conifers were some of the earliest trees.

12 This looks like beautiful embroidery, but it is a piece of fossilized coral.

13 These fossils are called 'sea lilies' but they are the remains of ancient sea creatures rather like starfish.

14 Sometimes, you can even find fossil footprints. This is the footprint of an early man.

Survival

1 These pictures are by a French engraver called Grandville. They illustrate the story of Robinson Crusoe which was written over 150 years ago by Daniel Defoe who was inspired by the real life adventures of an English sailor called Selkirk. Here you can see Robinson Crusoe just after he had been washed up on a desert island when his ship was wrecked in a storm.

2 Robinson Crusoe spent his first night on the island in a tree, as he was afraid of being attacked by wild animals.

3 After a few days, he had built himself a raft. He sailed out to the wreck and rescued some food, tools and other useful things.

Living on a desert island: Robinson Crusoe

After a huge storm at sea, Robinson Crusoe was washed up by the waves onto the shore of a small deserted island in the South Seas. Everyone else had drowned and there was no-one to rescue him. He had to work out for himself how he was going to survive. Even if you have never been a castaway, it is fun to play the 'survival game' and to imagine what life would be like. What would you do first?

The most important thing to find is fresh water. It is strange to think that, surrounded by sea, you still need fresh water. Did you know that in a hot climate you can only live for a day or so without anything to drink? But you can survive without any food for ten days or more.

When you explore your island, you may be lucky enough to find a stream or a lake, or even a little spring. A patch of green plants growing in a very dry place would tell you that there must be water just below the surface. You could dig down a little way to find it, like the Australian aborigines do in the desert. You could also collect rainwater in empty coconut shells or large, broad leaves.

On a Pacific island, the easiest food to find would be mangoes, pawpaws, pineapples, breadfruit and, of course bananas and coconuts. Coconuts are delicious and, as well as the flesh, they contain a good

4 When he had finished all the food from the ship,he made himself a hook and learned to fish in a little bay on the island.

5 He began to grow corn, using the bag of seed he had rescued from the wreck. He saved some of the grain to sow as seed the next year.

6 He soon felt lonely with no-one to talk to, so he caught a wild parrot, which he called Poll.

7 He tamed some other animals to keep him company and he shared his meals with them.

8 Then, one day he found a footprint in the sand. Now he knew he was not alone on the island.

drink of coconut milk. After a while, you might want a change from fruit and nuts so you could try fishing with a net made from woven creepers. There would be shellfish, like lobsters and crayfish and even turtles. You could trap birds or small animals, such as monkeys and wild pigs, for their skins and fur, as well as for their meat.

To cook your food, you need a fire. Robinson Crusoe had a *tinderbox*, an early sort of lighter, but you could try hitting two flints together to make a spark. If there were no flints on your island, you would have to rub two dry sticks together until they become hot enough to smoulder. This is very hard work, as you will find if you try it!

Like Robinson Crusoe, you would need a shelter from the hot sun and the heavy rain showers. You could build yourself a hut from a frame of strong sticks covered with a thatch of grasses or thick leaves.

But how would you like to be all by yourself with no-one to talk to? It might be quite fun for a few days, but you would soon get very lonely. Robinson Crusoe kept a pet parrot for company, but this was not the same as having a real person to talk to. In fact, he was very unhappy until he met Man Friday. Then, life was better. After all, you have probably discovered that a difficult thing is much easier and more fun to do if you have someone to help you.

9 He followed the footprints and found a young man from a nearby island. He called the man Friday, as that was the day he found him.

10 Together they built a sailing boat to escape from the island, but just when it was almost finished, a ship came to rescue them.

A pinch pot 1 Roll a piece of clay into a large ball and then, holding it firmly, press your thumbs into the middle. Continue pressing with your thumbs to hollow out your pot.

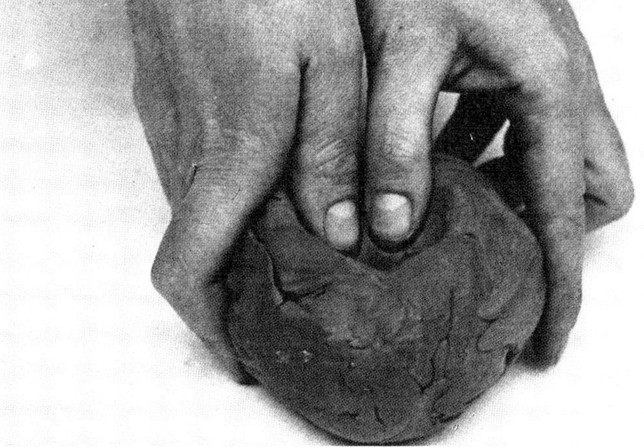

2 Smooth the outside with your palms. If you like, paint your pot or scratch a pattern on it with a stick. Now leave it to dry and harden in the sun.

Making pots

Why not make some of the pots that Robinson Crusoe made? He used clay which he dug out of the ground; you may not be able to do that, but you can buy clay from an art shop. Remember to keep the clay damp while you are working with it. To finish your pot, you should bake it in a kiln - a special oven – but if you can't, leave it in the sun to harden and dry. Making pots is not easy the first time, but with practice you can make pots of all shapes and sizes.

A coil pot 1 Shape some clay into a round, flat piece for the base.

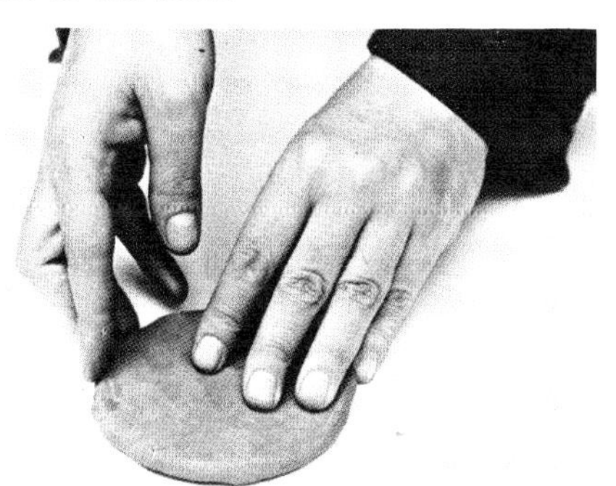

2 Roll another piece of clay into several long sausages.

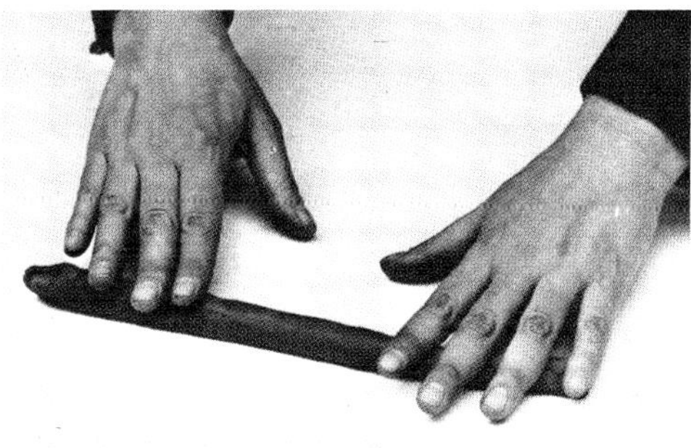

3 Fix the first sausage to the base and coil it round.

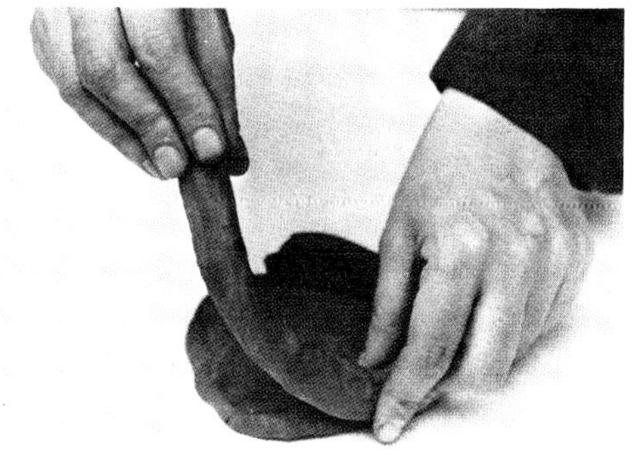

4 Join on another sausage and continue winding the clay round in a spiral, adding extra sausages as you need them.

5 When your pot is the size you want, smooth it down on the outside with your thumbs and leave it to dry out.

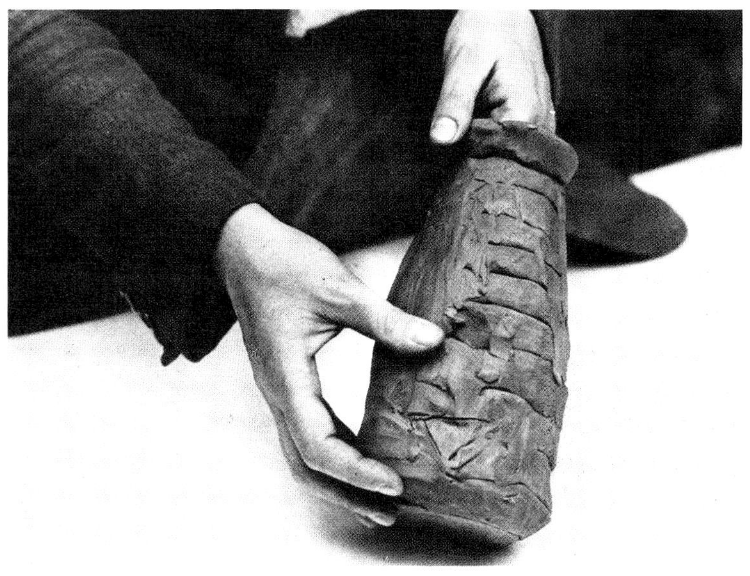

1 On the sea shore you will find all kinds of food, just as early man would have done: shellfish, and even seaweed, which in many countries is considered a great delicacy.

Beachcombing

Early man often lived on the sea shore, because there he found food and sometimes caves for shelter. If you go beachcombing, you will find all sorts of interesting things, although some of them, early man would *not* have discovered, like the bits and pieces washed from ships.

In rock pools, you will find darting shrimps, looking like tiny brown fish, and other shellfish, like mussels, whelks and winkles; but do be careful to ask an adult before you try eating them. Early man knew which ones were poisonous!

2 Jeremy has discovered mussels left behind by the tide.

3 Natasha has discovered a handful of different kinds of shellfish. You have to be certain *which* kinds are good to eat!

4 Kieran is picking up little crabs; but they look too small to eat yet.

5 Jeremy, Kieran and Robert are beachcombing after a storm.

6 Tiny crabs washed up by the waves, are now escaping back to the sea.

7 These tiny lobsters have been trapped in a rock pool.

The best time for beachcombing is after a storm. Then the waves will have thrown up bits of wood, shells and all kinds of treasure. In some places, people used timbers from wrecked ships to build their houses.

Waves can carry things for hundreds of miles. Perhaps you will find a bottle with a message in it, sent from someone in another country. Perhaps you will just find tiny pieces of wave-worn glass. But one thing is certain. With every tide there will be a new collection of strange discoveries for you to make.

8 Everyone can play the beachcombing game, whether they need to find food to live on or whether they are just doing it for fun. ▶

1 Some children, aged 9-11, went on a 'survival trip' in a wood and drew both what they discovered and also what they would like to have found.

The survival game

Even if you are not on a desert island, you can still play the survival game. Who knows? One day you may need to know how to live out-of-doors.

First of all, you will need food. Try to identify some wild food plants - checking, of course, with an adult that you have found the right ones. In spring and summer, you can pick many kinds of leaves for salads - dandelions for example. You can even make soup from young nettles (they do not sting after they are cooked). In autumn, there is more to find: sweet chestnuts, blackberries, wild strawberries, hazelnuts and mushrooms. *Take extra care with all kinds of fungi, because some are very poisonous.*

Then you can make a camp out of leaves and branches. This is how early man lived. He would stay just as long as he could find food and then he would move on to another temporary camp. He knew how to tell by the tiniest signs which animals were near and how to track them down. He even knew which bird cries were alarm signals. This kind of skill comes from a life-time in the wild but, if you keep your eyes open, you can discover lots of interesting things in just one day.

2 Olivia, aged 11, painted a picture of the wild raspberries and strawberries that she found.

3 Charles, aged 10, found a stream with fish in it, but he did not have a net.

4 Joanna, Anthony and Sarah, aged 10, found mushrooms and wild apple trees.

5 Patrick, aged 11, painted an imaginary palm tree. This boy is climbing for the coconuts.

6 More wild apple trees painted by 9-year-old Stephen.

7 Laura, aged 9, painted little mushrooms and wild raspberries.

8 Harriet, aged 9, painted herself, Penny and Julie picking blackberries and wild raspberries.

The origins of man

1 In some parts of Indonesia, people still live very much like the earliest farmers. This is the island of Bali, where nowadays aeroplanes land every day with hundreds of tourists; but these young herdsmen still take their geese out to the hillside to graze as their ancestors must have done.

2 These Red Indians from Utah, in North America, are grazing their flocks of sheep.

3 In Tunisia, some farmers still use the kind of plough invented in prehistoric times.

The beginning of agriculture

When early man first began to grow things for himself, it was probably the most important discovery he ever made. Suddenly, his whole way of life changed. Instead of moving about all the time, looking for food, he stayed in one place.

It is quite difficult to catch a wild chicken or to gather enough grains of corn to make a loaf of bread. Think how much easier it is to have chickens in your yard and a field full of corn. More food fed more people; and the population of the world increased faster than ever before - and it is still increasing today. Villages grew up for the first time. Now that a family had a settled home, they could begin to collect possessions. If you have to carry everything around with you, you tend to keep only a few belongings. Living in a house, you begin to have more. Some people believe that this was when we first began to make wars on each other: one village wanted to own its neighbour's fields and animals.

How did it all begin? Perhaps when someone was gathering wild barley and wheat grains, she dropped a few on the ground and noticed that they grew. Next year, she planted some on purpose to see what would happen. Meanwhile, someone else might have caught and tamed some young goats and calves.

Perhaps the most amazing thing about the growth of agriculture is what it meant for man himself: he began to take control of his surroundings. It was the beginning of the modern age.

◀ 4 Today, we usually thresh corn (separate the grains from the husks and straw) by machinery. But in Sicily, some farmers still thresh their corn with wooden flails.

5 Here in Ethiopia, grain is still ground into flour by pounding it in stone querns with smooth stone pestles. ▶

1,2,3,4 These are little female statues from the stone age. We believe that they were ancient symbols of fertility; our ancestors believed that they had the power to help women to have children, and also to make the crops grow better. 1 and 2 come from France, 3 from Ecuador and 4 from Hungary.

Farming changed our lives

People now began inventing more and more tools and weapons to help look after their new fields and flocks. One good idea led to another, and soon they were making all kinds of baskets and cooking pots, polished flint knives and sickles for cutting the corn, simple carts for carrying things from one place to another; and even a plough. In many parts of the world today, people still use the same kind of plough that these early farmers invented.

It was at this time that people began organizing village life. Both men and women already shared the work, but now jobs were divided amongst everyone. One family would paint and make jewellery; another would look after the animals; yet another would make pots or baskets. We know this from the pictures, carvings and tools we have discovered.

5 A well was very important to every village because it gave a constant supply of fresh water. This one was dug at Byblos, in the Lebanon.

6 These are querns for grinding corn into flour, also found at Byblos, in the Lebanon.

1 There are many different sorts of plants. Some have long roots, some short, some have tubers (like potatoes) and some have big green leaves. Often, they take up different kinds of food from the soil.

How plants grow

What makes a plant grow? Early farmers soon found that they needed to do more than simply drop the seeds into the ground. Nearly all plants need water and sunlight, but they also need a fertile soil, rather like humans need vitamins. Soil planted with the same crop, year after year, soon loses its goodness and the plants grow weak and spindly. Much later, people discovered that if they planted *different* crops, the soil stayed fertile. But from the earliest times, people knew that some plants can help each other: garlic is still planted in vineyards to keep the grapes healthy.

Early farmers learnt that to have a good harvest *next* year, they must choose grain from the fattest, strongest ears of corn to use as seed. In this way, plants slowly changed. All the flowers and vegetables we grow now had wild ancestors - like briar roses, wild plums and crab apples.

Today, farmers are still experimenting: they are even growing new plants that never existed before! But 'improvements' are not always for the best. Some plant sprays used for controlling insects and diseases can be dangerous to humans and animals. All living things depend on each other - this is the balance of nature - and it takes thousands of years to undo the damage if it is disturbed.

2 Some plants like the shade, some like sunshine. Here you can see how one plant can protect another.

1 A marmot on the look-out, giving its high-pitched whistle of alarm.

Animals need their own space

All living things need space. They need it to build their homes, to look after their babies and to find their food. Even plants need room to grow. For this reason, most animals mark out a territory, which they protect against intruders.

You have probably seen sparrows quarrelling in the springtime. This is because one sparrow has tried to trespass into another's territory. But even though they try to look as fierce as possible, animals of the same kind rarely kill each other. It is enough that the trespasser has been thoroughly frightened! Some animals who live in groups, like marmots or rabbits, even post look-outs to warn of enemies approaching their territory.

2 While look-outs keep watch, the other marmots can eat in peace or play games together.

Man, too, has his territory

Human beings are territorial. They mark out their own spaces and defend them too, against intruders. In fact, we often protect ourselves as carefully from each other as from our natural enemies. Haven't you seen notices saying *Strictly private. Keep out*?

But this does not mean that humans want to fight all the time. It simply shows that humans, just like animals, need their own space. We, too, tend to put on a threatening display when we see trespassers.

In fact, above everything, humans are *co-operative*. We like doing things in groups. If we really were so aggressive, we would never have been able to organize ourselves at all. We would probably never have come out of the primeval forests.

1 Humans protect their territories, just as animals do. This is the border between Spanish territory and Morocco, patrolled by guards.

2 These stone walls in Italy were made by an ancient civilization to mark out the division between one owner's field and another's.

1 Today, hunting is not so necessary as it once was. The Rajah in this Indian miniature is chasing animals simply for sport. But before early people settled and became farmers, hunting was one of the first ways in which we co-operated together to find food.

2 For these African bushmen, hunting is still an important part of their lives. This magic ceremony is to help them make a good catch.

3 This man has skilfully disguised himself with ostrich feathers so that he can creep up on his catch.

How man became a hunter

Compared to a sabre-toothed tiger, or a mammoth, a human being was weak and defenceless; but he had some weapons that were stronger than any of theirs. He knew how to learn, how to co-operate with other men and how to use his surroundings.

Organized hunting was a very important step in man's progress. It meant that he worked in a group and pooled his discoveries.

Hunting gave humans the reason to invent better weapons - polished stone axes, spears and arrow-heads - and they learned to set traps and to follow animals by their tracks. Then, when he had caught them, he learned to use their skins and teeth to make clothes and more weapons and tools.

Man's ability to live in a group and co-operate together was beginning to give him a big advantage over other animals. Instead of being hunted, he had become the hunter.

5 Argentinian Indians hunting a condor with sticks.

◀ 4 Like some early hunters, this African uses a 'propellor' to throw his spear with greater force.

1 Kerry and Samantha are staying on a small farm in the country. Here they are by the henhouse. Kerry is giving a piece of bread to Mrs Chuck, her favourite hen. Today they want to explore.

2 Samantha decides to take her camera so they can play a kind of hunting game; but the animals will be caught on film and not in a net. Sukie, the white goat won't turn round to look at the camera; Nanette, her kid, is too greedy to think of anything else but her next meal.

Looking after our animals

Today, man kills animals for many different reasons, not only for food. Sometimes he kills them because they are a nuisance to him; they eat his crops, they damage his land. He kills them by destroying the places where they live, because he wants to live there himself. He also kills them for their furs and feathers, which he can sell at a high price.

It is strange and rather frightening to think that soon, unless we do something to stop it, you will only be able to see certain kinds of whale or tiger, seal or deer, in a book like this, or perhaps in a zoo. The animals themselves will never be seen in the wild again because, like the dodo, they will be extinct.

Is this important? From the beginning of life on earth, animals have died out. But today, man is destroying the places where animals live so thoroughly that not only *one* animal dies, a whole group are threatened. Forests which have existed for millions of years are now disappearing at the rate of fifty acres a minute. If we take care now, the animals could still survive. Otherwise, it may be too late.

3 Next, they see Baffy, the cat, lying on a rug in the sun. Eyes half closed, he is playing with a wasp. "Oh Baffy!" shouts Kerry, "it'll sting you!" And she picks him up.

4 Baffy wakes up. He is cross at being taken away from his game. His tail flicks from side to side, and before Samantha can get the camera ready properly, he is off.

◀ **5** It is lunch time at the pigsty and the mother pig is quite worn out with all her squeaking babies. "Look at little Curly," says Kerry, "he's always late for lunch."

6 Outside the barn they see the grey goose, who wants to find out what they are doing. But she doesn't notice the three little ducklings following her. ▶

7 The ducklings have slipped away from their brothers and sisters. Perhaps they are off to explore. Here comes another duck and her sister, trying to make sure that none of the family wanders off.

8 When you are duckling-size, the farm is very big and there are lots of places to hide. They can't see past the enormous legs of the bullocks, but they do see the nice puddle their hooves have made in the mud.

9 "One, two, three - bother - One, two, three, four - where are the others?" says the mother duck. It is not easy to count ducklings.

10 There they are, hiding in the grass after their swim. They are very pleased with themselves.

11 On the way back to the henhouse, Kerry collects some corn from the barn so they can feed all the chickens. There is a great deal of squabbling and clucking because everyone feels sure that they are not getting a fair share.

12 Blackie, the old black hen, makes such a fuss that Kerry picks her up. "It's not going to be your *last* meal ever!" she says. Blackie gives her a hopeful peck. Perhaps she has some corn left? Somewhere?

13 In the field they see Snowdrop, the beautiful white rabbit. She is busy eating and Kerry and Samantha creep up on her quietly.

14 But they needn't have worried. Snowdrop is far too interested in the fresh green grass to mind beng caught.

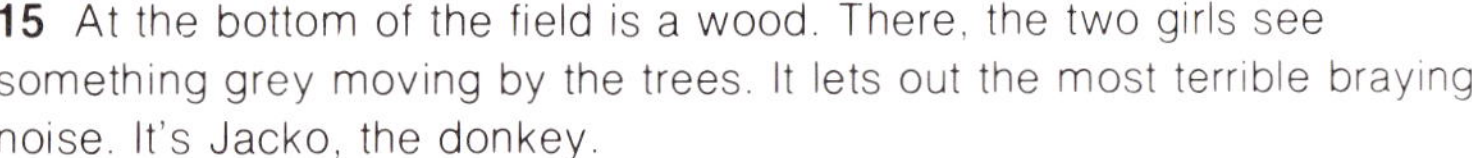

15 At the bottom of the field is a wood. There, the two girls see something grey moving by the trees. It lets out the most terrible braying noise. It's Jacko, the donkey.

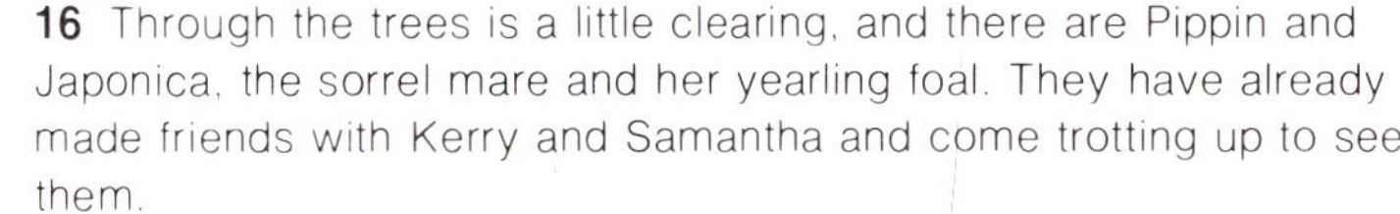

16 Through the trees is a little clearing, and there are Pippin and Japonica, the sorrel mare and her yearling foal. They have already made friends with Kerry and Samantha and come trotting up to see them.

17 "Tea time for us," says Kerry, when they have said goodbye to the ponies. Suddenly, they see a strange animal in the long grass. It's a polecat!

18 He has been tamed by one of the farm helpers so he even lets the girls pick him up. "He smells a bit funny!" says Kerry.

19 "Perhaps he's cold," suggests Samantha, and wraps him up in her sweater.

20 But the polecat gets bored with playing. He jumps onto Kerry's lap, curls up and pretends to go to sleep.

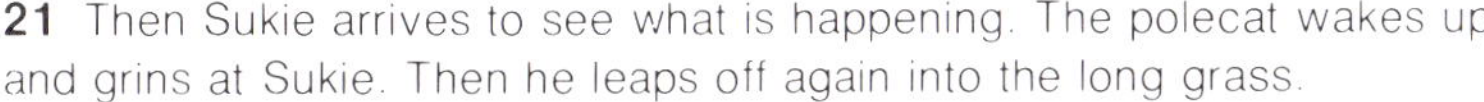

21 Then Sukie arrives to see what is happening. The polecat wakes up and grins at Sukie. Then he leaps off again into the long grass.

22 But before he goes, he turns round to give the girls one last look. "He's saying goodbye," says Kerry. "It really *is* time for tea."

The discovery of fire

Can you imagine what the world would be like without fire? There would be no heat and no light, except when the sun was shining, and all our food would be raw. There would be no cars, no machinery and no industry. Fire was one of man's great discoveries, made maybe a million years before he became a farmer.

How did he find it? It is impossible to tell now; we can only guess. Perhaps he took a burning branch from a forest fire, maybe he stole some hot ash from a volcano, or maybe he watched a tree struck by lightning. It must have taken a lot of courage in those early days to pick up fire. Even today, most people can feel that there is something almost like magic about an open fire as it crackles and burns.

1 Perhaps men first took fire from the hot ash from volcanoes.

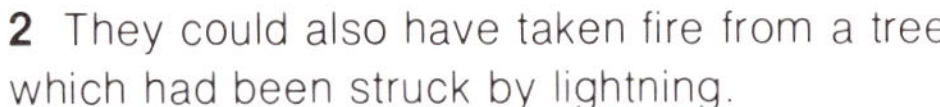

2 They could also have taken fire from a tree which had been struck by lightning.

Until early man knew how to make fire himself, it was vital that someone should make sure that the camp fire was burning safely all the time. You can imagine how important this job was. Fire meant that people could sit round talking together when it was dark and cold. Fire frightened away wild animals. Fire was always at the centre of early ceremonies and rituals. Even today, a flame can symbolize life to us, and there are special flames kept burning to remind us of our past. The Olympic torch is passed from country to country, as a symbol of friendship between nations.

Strangely enough, although there are hundreds of myths from all over the world about the discovery of fire, nearly all of them

3 Then they discovered how to make fire whenever they needed it: by rubbing two dry sticks together.

4 Another way of fire-making was to hit two flints together to make a spark.

agree that a high price had to be paid for it. A myth from Greece describes how human beings were made by a god called Prometheus, who was very proud of his creations and loved them dearly. One day, he decided to give them fire, because it was the best gift he knew. He went to Zeus, the king of the gods, to beg for it; but the other gods had become jealous of men and were afraid that if they had fire, they would become *too* clever. "No," said Zeus. "You must *never* give them fire."

Prometheus went away and saw his people shivering in the cold. Suddenly, he made up his mind. In the middle of the night, he stole fire from Mount Olympus and carried it down to mankind. Zeus was furious when he discovered what had happened and punished Prometheus savagely. He was chained for centuries to a rock, where every day he was attacked by a huge eagle. Every evening, his wounds would heal, to be slashed open again the following day. Mankind was punished too. Zeus sent them a box, full of all the evils we know today - Envy, Sickness, Anger, Fear, Pain - and one of the first humans, called Pandora, opened the box in a fit of curiosity and let them out. According to the story, Hope was also in the box, and that is why it is often all we have left when everything goes wrong!

So, all those years ago, man knew that although fire is beautiful and useful, it is also dangerous and destructive.

1 8-year-old Anna painted this huge forest fire which has turned the sky red.

2 Denny, aged 10, drew these four volcanoes.

3 Claire, aged 9, painted a bonfire.

Fire is beautiful - and dangerous

Fire can make things clean. This sounds odd, but it is true, because fire destroys germs and dirt. Years ago, a small fire started in a baker's shop in the city of London. It soon spread, until it destroyed nearly the whole city. It was almost a disaster - but not quite. For generations, people had died of disease because of overcrowding and dirt. Once the fire had made a clean space, the people who were left had a chance to make a new start.

Controlled burning is nature's way of destroying all the dead wood which chokes the new young

4 Colin, aged 7, and Ruth, aged 12, painted a camp fire.

5 Molten lava from a volcano in a collage by Dave, aged 8.

6 These hunters, painted by Neil, aged 8, are frightening a mammoth with their burning spears.

plants. It also covers the ground with fertile ash. Even more important, it means that a huge fire, which destroys everything, is much more unlikely.

So fire is necessary; but if it is to be useful, and not dangerous, it must be very carefully controlled. It is also beautiful as the flames leap and dance, orange, yellow, red and white. Why not try to paint it, as these children have done?

7 Here is a prehistoric scene, painted by Philip and Leroy, aged 8, and Winston, aged 7.

◀ **1** These Amazon Indians use poisonous plants called *magic fish* to stun the fish, which they can then catch easily.

3 Fishing in a group, in India. Fine mesh nets are lowered gently into the water so that the fish are not frightened away. ▼

2 Fishing with a *sucker fish* in Somalia. These fish stick onto other fish which are then caught.

When man moved from place to place

Before man learned to live in settled groups, he was what we call a hunter-gatherer. He travelled through forests and open grassland in small bands of about twenty, picking roots and berries and catching a few animals and fish, just like the few remaining hunter-gatherers do to this day.

Like these people, early men probably lived surprisingly well. They had lots of leisure time to visit other tribes, when they could swap news, arrange marriages, dance and sing. Hunting played a special part in tribal life, because it brought everyone together. When there was a kill, it would be shared, because one hunter could not eat a whole bison! You can imagine the excitement of the band after a successful hunt and the pride of the man who had made the kill. All the same, we think that early man probably ate less meat than nuts and berries, which were gathered by the women. Perhaps they were responsible for a very important invention: the bag. Without it, people would still have had to eat where they found food. They could not have brought it home to cook.

By now, people were talking. They had words for 'good' and 'bad', and for their tools, animals and the food they ate; they had to. They were learning fast, and language helped them to share their discoveries.

4 These Australian aborigines are searching for roots and berries. It needs many years of experience to know *which* are good to eat.

5 Experience tells: this African bushman from the Kalahari has discovered some wild onions.

How we once lived

Backwards in time

I told you before how, one hot afternoon, we travelled back in time to rescue Mikko, our dog, who had been sent who-knows-where by an incredible time machine. This is what happened.

We were sitting there, a bit shaken by the upside-down, giddy feeling of time travelling, when a boy and a girl of about our age ran past. They didn't see us. Running behind them, barking his head off, was Mikko.

"Let's follow them!" said Sam, straightaway, and running down a path between huge fir trees, we almost bumped into them both. We were all so surprised, we just stared at each other. Then Mikko ran towards us, wagging his tail.

"Mikko!" Sam yelled. "Where have you been?" Mikko licked our hands, whining with excitement. The girl smiled and said something I didn't understand. It seemed to be a question, so I smiled too and said, "I'm Charlotte and this is Sam. What's your name?" The boy came forward and touched our clothes. You could see he was quite amazed by us. I suppose it must have been very odd for them; after all, *we* knew we'd been time travelling, but they couldn't possibly know where we'd come from. The girl made a sign for us to go with them, but Sam wasn't sure. "Maybe it's a trap," he said.

"No, it isn't," I said. "See they're just like us. They look really friendly; and anyway, we've got the clock, so we can go home any time we like." Saying that about the clock changed his mind and so we set off, the two strangers in front, talking away, and us coming along behind.

"Do you know," said Sam, softly, "I think I know where we are!" He always has a good sense of direction.

"Where?" I said.

"We're back near the cave where we found the pictures," he said, triumphantly, "only things are a bit different." He was right; but the countryside was greener and there were fir trees everywhere. Soon we came to the mouth of a cave. I didn't recognise it, but Sam whispered "It's our cave; only when we saw it before, the way in was more blocked up."

A man with thick brown hair came out of the

cave. He was wearing a sort of tunic made from skins. Suddenly, I felt scared. What if he didn't like us? What if the time thing went wrong and we couldn't get back? But our new friends ran over to him and started telling him something - about us, I suppose and Mikko, because there was a lot of pointing. The man smiled and beckoned and we all went into the cave, which smelled very strongly of people.

Two women were sitting round a big open fire and a warm, cooking smell was coming from somewhere. It was cold outside, and very different from our sunny back garden and I was hungry. Sam said, "Can we have something to eat?" and he pointed to his mouth. Sam doesn't care where he is, he just goes straight to the point. One of the women laughed and pulled out a smoking-hot package from the ashes round the fire.

"What's *that*?" said Sam.

The woman opened the dusty, black-looking bundle and passed us a couple of lumps of meat. Sam took a bite.

"Mmmm!" he said. "Try a bit." And I did. Who could have guessed that buried meat would taste so good?

Then the boy handed us a couple of tunics, like the ones everyone seemed to be wearing. The girl pointed to herself and said, "Susa," and the boy said "Mur". We said our names again. It is amazing how well you can understand someone even if you don't know their language.

Susa and Mur showed us their new slings, which looked very simple, and in their hands were very accurate. Sam and I were hopeless at first, but we got better with practice. It is surprisingly hard, if you have ever tried.

All of a sudden, Mikko came racing into the cave and hid behind Sam's legs. "What's the matter?" said Sam.

A couple of men were running up the slope towards the cave. They looked really scared. Mur frowned and put one hand up to his head and pretended to charge at us. He looked rather funny; but we could see that whatever it was, it was nothing to laugh at. There was a terrible squealing noise and we all rushed to the mouth of the cave. Charging across the grass was the hairiest, angriest-looking rhino I have ever seen. Mur yelled out loud and raised his fist. Sam and I understood straightaway what he meant: we were going on a hunt!

The great hunt

Susa and Mur grabbed a handful of smooth, round pebbles and tucked them into the pouches at their belts. They already had their slings in their hands. Sam and I still had slings and stones from our practice.

Just below us, the rhino was charging at a group of men. I couldn't understand it; they seemed to be *encouraging* him to attack them. To one side, crouching with a spear in his hand, was the man angry rhino.

There was a shout of horror from the men. The rhino had changed direction and now he was attacking them from the side. Our friends' father was right in his path. Mur and Susa ran screaming down from the cave, trying to distract the rhino. Then Sam was running and shouting for all he was worth and I found myself screaming too. It was all terribly confused. Mikko was barking at our ankles.

who had invited us into the cave. He was Susa and Mur's father, I think. Then, in a flash, I saw what was happening: the other men were leading the rhino into some sort of trap, where he could be speared. But they must have had no fear at all to do that. Their only weapons were sticks and stones and I don't suppose that even a man with a big shotgun would have felt very brave so close to that huge,

All of a sudden, he dashed out, past me and Sam, past Susa and Mur. Everyone stared as our small, white dog, snarling like a whole pack of wolfhounds instead of the fox terrier he is, went straight for the rhino.

The rhino stopped dead in his tracks and glowered at Mikko out of his red, piggy eyes. Mikko was jumping around so fast that you could see the big animal was thoroughly confused. He didn't know who to attack, the dog or the men. Then, as quickly as he'd run out, Mikko made a dash for safety, tail between his legs. That did it. The rhino charged. With a great yell, Mur and Susa started to run towards the higher ground and I saw their plan. They would be *above* the rhino, and they would have a perfect target for their slings.

Sam and I panted after them. It was all so sudden and I didn't have time to think what would happen if the rhino changed direction as he had done before. . . .

Mikko streaked past just below us; then the rhino came thundering after him. Susa and Mur took aim with their slings. Shaking a bit, Sam and I did too, and we all fired together.

I screamed as the huge rhino crashed to the ground, blood streaming from its head. Mur and Susa went wild with excitement. They ran to the animal and cut off a lump of its hairy coat and waved it in the air, shouting and laughing. I just shook.

"It's all right," said Sam, white as a sheet. "It's dead."

"I know," I said, and sat down on the grass with a bump. Some of the hunters came up and hugged

Susa and Mur and patted us on the shoulder; but as for Mikko, he was the hero of the hour. Everyone hugged him.

We all went back to the cave and, on the way, I started giggling.

"What is it?" said Sam.

"It's Mikko," I said. "After hunting rhinos, we'll never get him back to chasing the cat next-door!"

The secret of the cave of mysteries

My legs were still shaking a bit when we got back to the cave. There were now about twenty people round the fire and everyone was talking and laughing at once. It was like a holiday. Someone put some flowers round Sam's neck and I saw Susa and Mur had blood running down their foreheads - not their blood, but the rhino's.

When the excitement had calmed down a little, Susa whispered something to Mur and he stared at them said anything; but Mur was chanting a strange, wavery little song that went up and down the same notes over and over again. Then he and Susa climbed a little way up the rocks and disappeared behind a big boulder. Sam looked at me and shrugged his shoulders. We followed them to the mouth of another cave, only this one was much narrower. One after another, we squeezed in, following Susa with the torch. There was a whimper

us. She was clearly asking him something. Then he grinned and took us outside.

Mur knelt down with two dry sticks and twirled one in the other. They began to smoke. He heaped a few dry leaves around them. I was amazed. I had never seen anyone make a fire like that before. The leaves burst into flame and Susa lit a sort of candle made of animal fat. It smelled terrible. Neither of and a clattering of claws and Mikko was at my ankles. He didn't want to be left out of anything.

As the cave opened out a little, Susa put a finger to her lips. Sam squeezed my hand.

"What is it?" I whispered.

"Maybe it's wild animals or something that lives here," said Sam, wisely. "Just follow Susa." So we did, and Mikko padded along at our heels.

We climbed into another cave with smooth, polished sides and a dark blue pool of water in the middle. There, on the walls, were the same incredible pictures of animals that we had seen last summer. Only this time, the colours glowed rich brown, red and yellow. They looked quite new. Sam and I stared at the leaping deer and galloping horses and huge bear-like creatures fighting.

Susa and Mur seemed to have forgotten all about it looked a bit wobbly because we were not used to the earth-paint which kept going lumpy and dry. Susa came and looked at our picture and she giggled a bit; and then we went to look at theirs. The rhino was really good, but I couldn't understand why they had drawn the people like sticks.

I was beginning to get shivery and I felt quite disappointed when Susa and Mur set off further into the cave. I wanted to get back; but soon I heard

us. They were talking to each other and mixing the coloured earth from the floor of the cave with water in a little hollowed-out stone. Then they began to paint a huge red and brown rhinoceros. They drew themselves, the other hunters and even Mikko.

"We must draw something, too," I said. "We must draw *our* pictures."

And so Sam and I drew ourselves in the hunt; but voices ahead of us. Then I could see the light of a fire and we found ourselves at the back of the main cave.

Everyone shouted and cheered when we arrived, and they did not seem a bit surprised to see us.

"Maybe," I thought, "everyone goes into that cave and draws a picture to show that they have made a big kill."

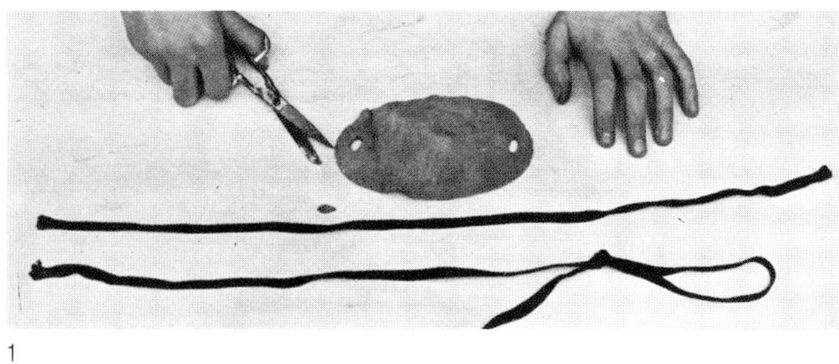

1

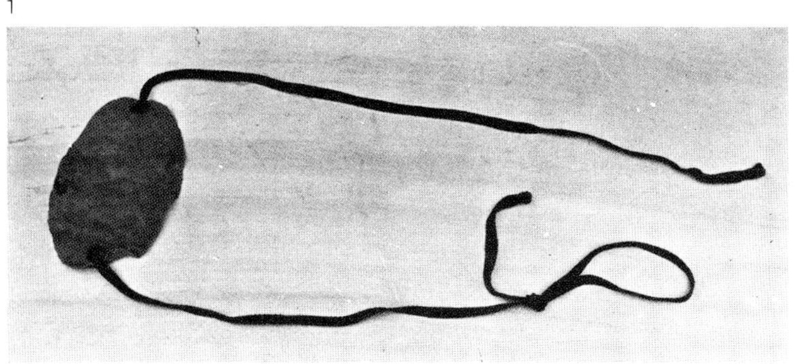

2

A sling 1 Find two bootlaces and tie a loop in one of them. Cut a piece of material, as you can see here.

2 Tie the cords to the material.

3 To use the sling, put your hand through the loop, load the sling with a conker and whirl it round over your head. Let go of the loose end of the string and the conker will fly out.

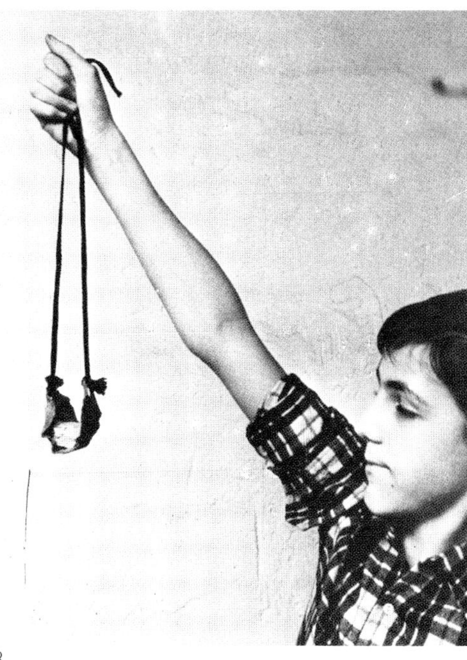

3

Making stone age tools

When early man first began to use tools and weapons, he had to use the materials he could find around him. He might pick up the nearest branch or throw a heavy stone to frighten away an animal or a stranger. Soon, he learned to improve these simple tools to make them more effective.

You can try making some of the tools stone age man used. All you will need are some sticks, stones and strips of leather (or string). You will soon find that it is quite hard to make these things properly: it takes skill to tie a stone to a stick firmly enough so that it will not fly off when the tool is used.

If you use the tools you have made, you *must* make sure that there are no people or animals around who could get hurt - after all, early man often used his slings and axes to kill.

1

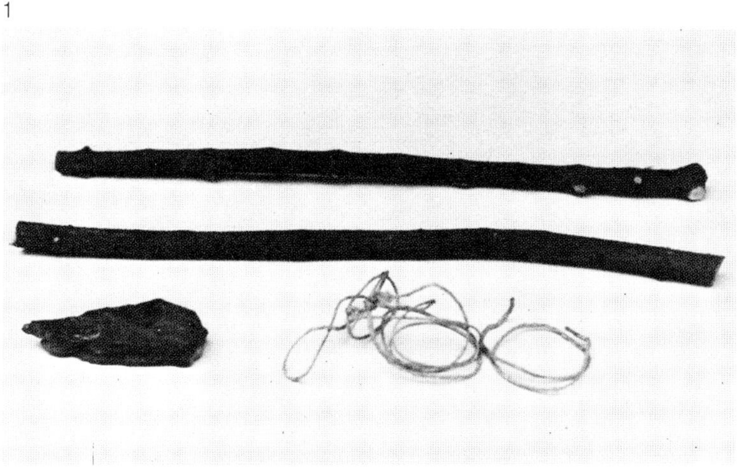

2

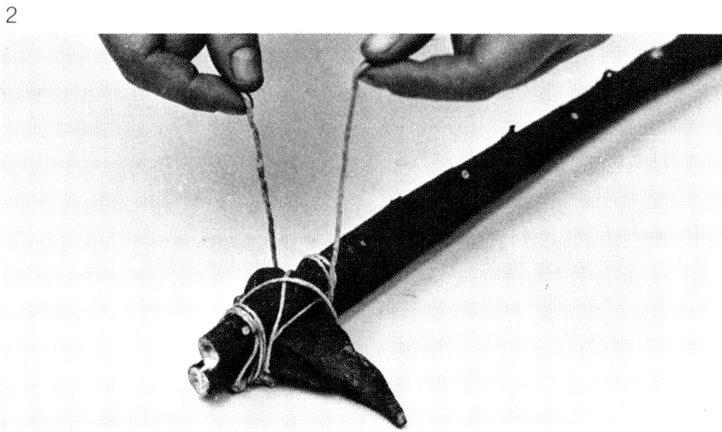

A small hoe 1 Collect two sticks, an old bootlace and a flat, pointed stone (a flint is often suitable).

2 Tie the stone firmly between the two sticks.

3 Then tie the two sticks together at the bottom. Now you have a hoe very like the ones the first farmers used.

3

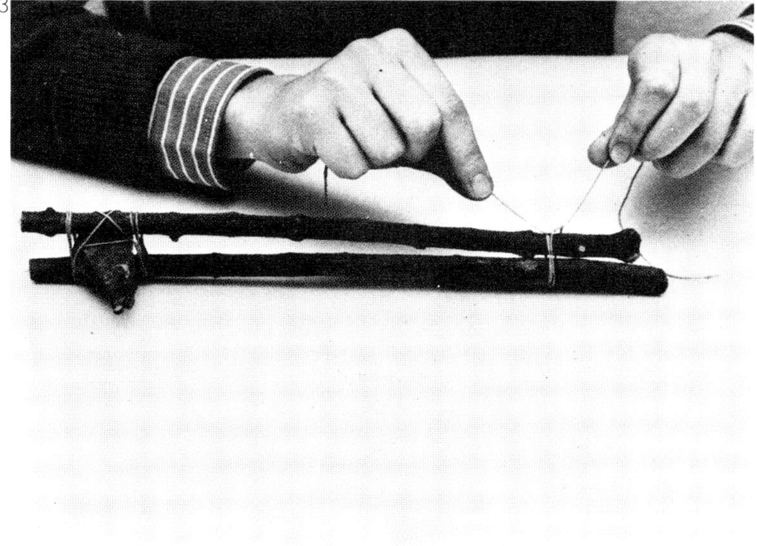

An axe 1 Saw about half a metre off a slim pole (an old broomstick would be ideal).

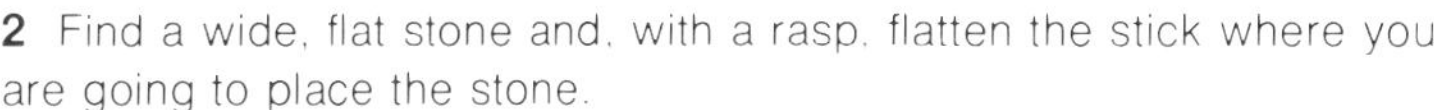

2 Find a wide, flat stone and, with a rasp, flatten the stick where you are going to place the stone.

3 Holding the stone firmly to the stick, start winding one end of the string round them, as shown.

4 To lash the stone tightly to the stick, you must wind the string crosswise, as you see here.

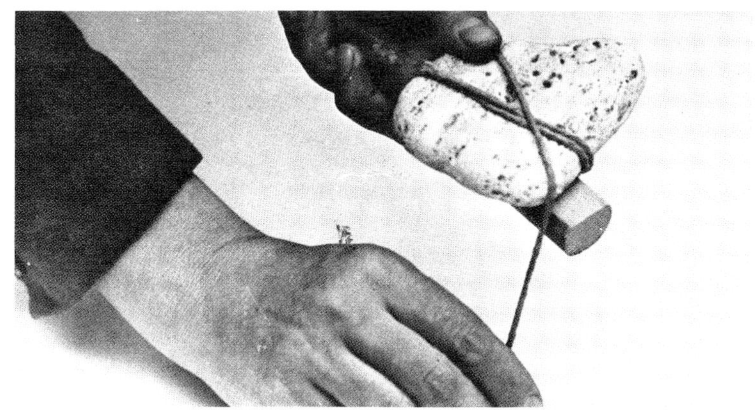

5 Then wind the string a few times between the stick and the stone.

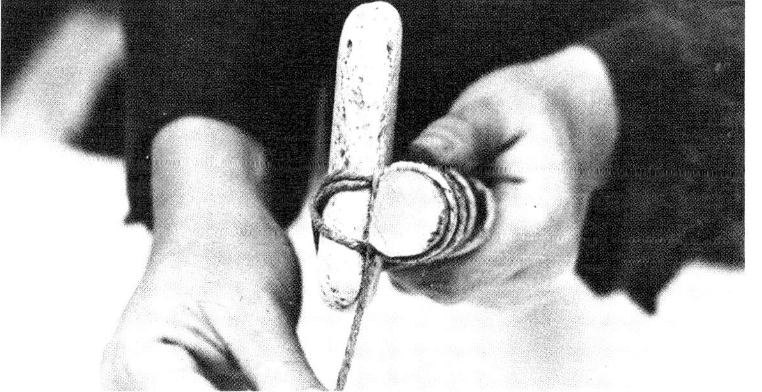

6 Tie the two ends of the string together firmly.

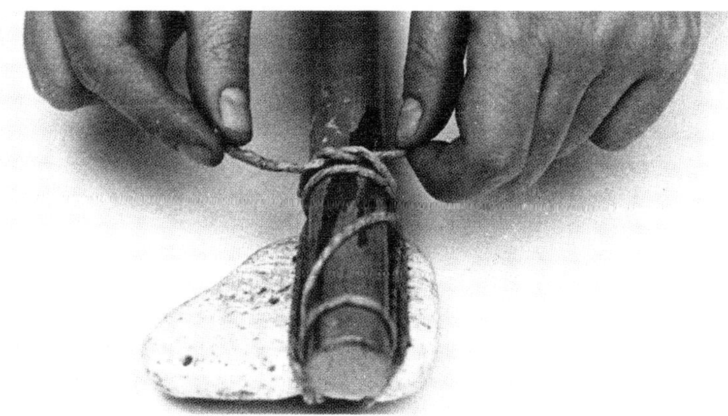

7 Prehistoric man went hunting with axes very like this one.

A shell necklace 1 With a piece of sandpaper, rub the end of a shell to make it thin at this point.

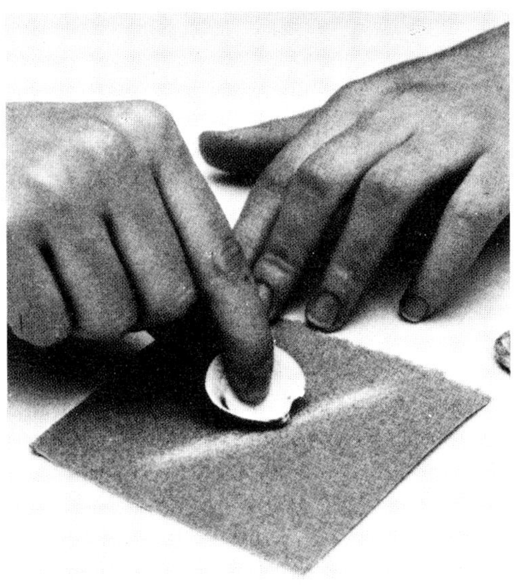

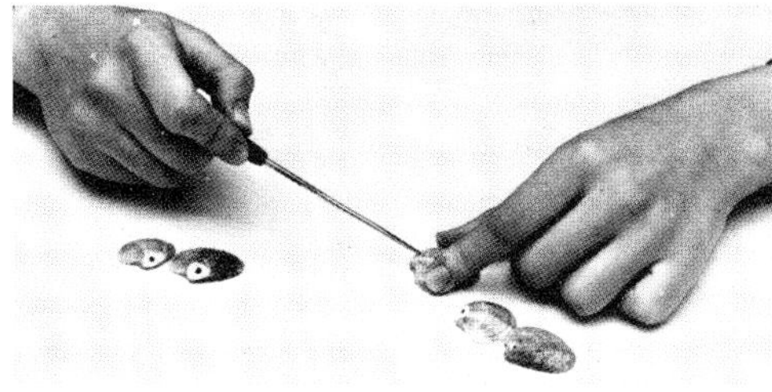

2 Then you can pierce a hole without breaking the shell.

3 Thread the shells one by one onto a string and tie the ends together.

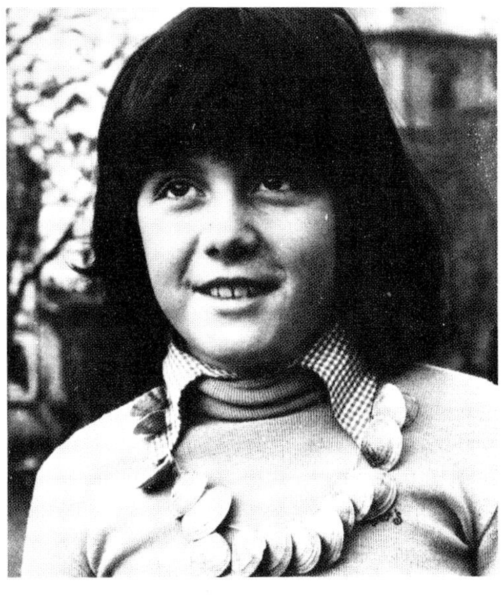

4 You can decorate your necklace by painting the shells with clear or coloured varnish.

A prehistoric comb 1 Arrange a row of long pointed sticks (like cocktail sticks) between four short ones, as shown.

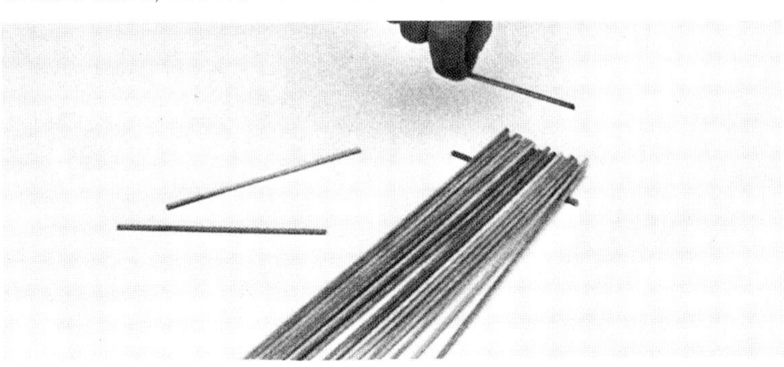

2 Tie the ends of the short sticks together firmly, to hold the long sticks in place.

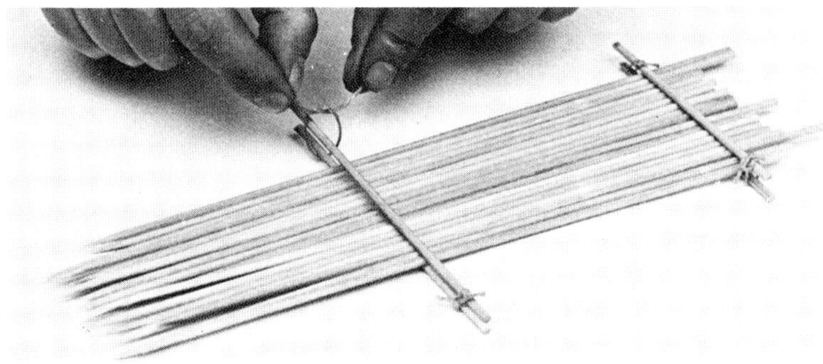

3 Weave a piece of string in and out across the sticks.

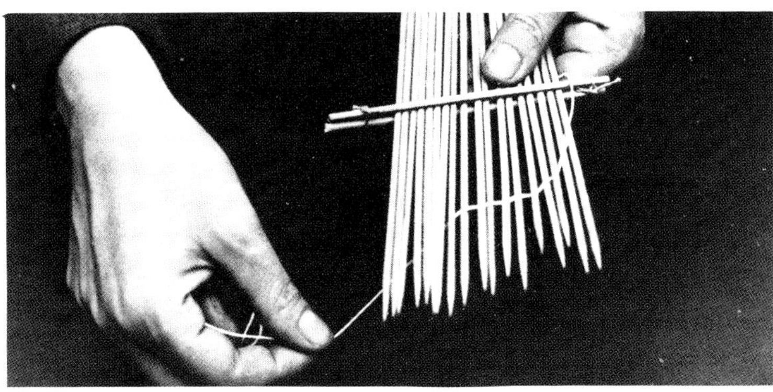

4 Continue to weave the string between the sticks, as shown, to hold them in place.

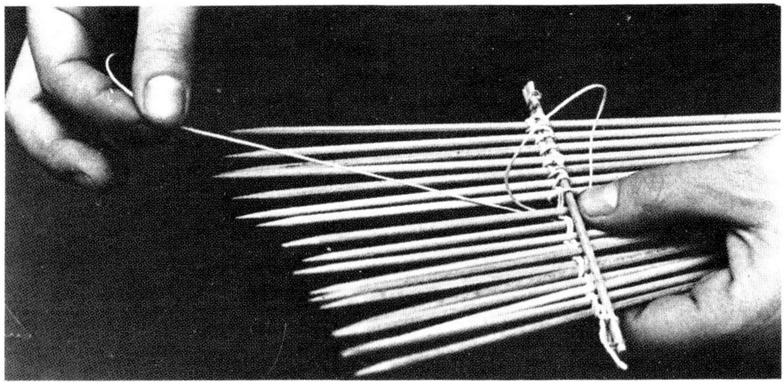

5 On the cross stick nearest the teeth of the comb, continue weaving so that the sticks are pushed further apart by the string.

6 This is a finished comb. Some tribespeople still make combs like this out of twigs.

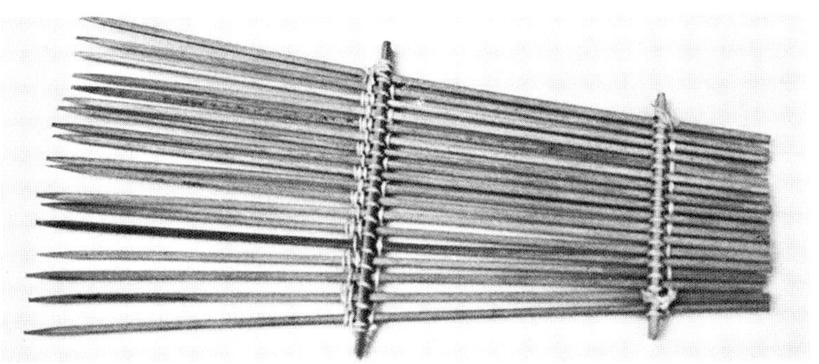

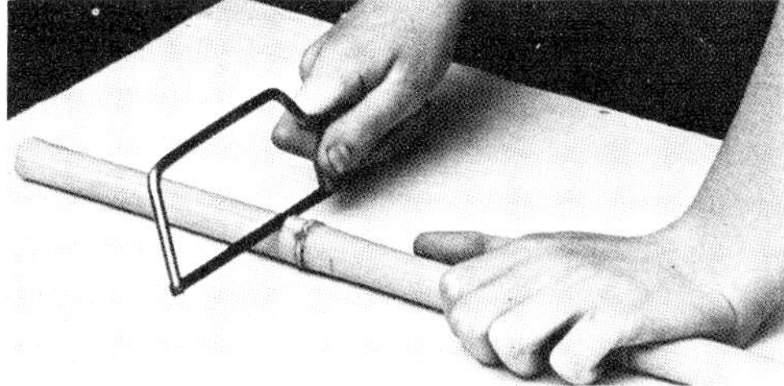

A bamboo flute 1 Cut diagonally a piece of bamboo about 20 cms long.

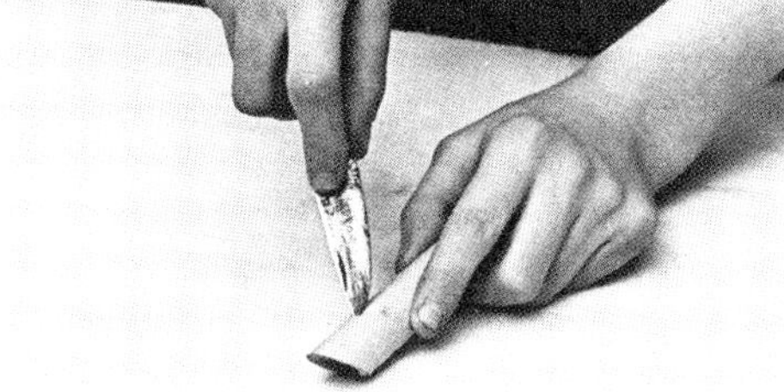

2 Carefully cut a few round holes with a pointed knife.

3 Cut a small round slice from a cork. Cut off one edge of the slice.

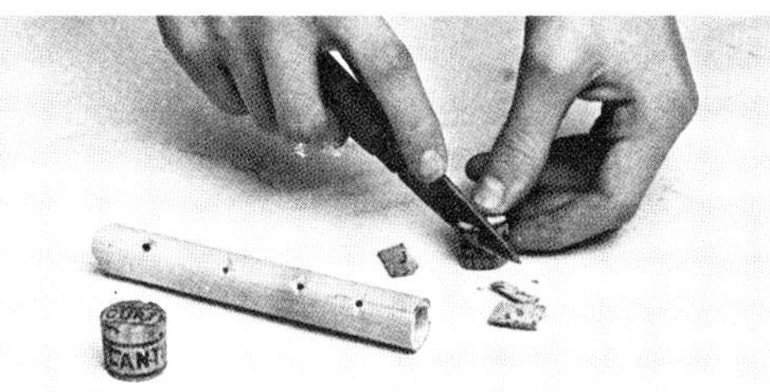

4 Push the cork into the end of the flute as far as you can and trim the end off.

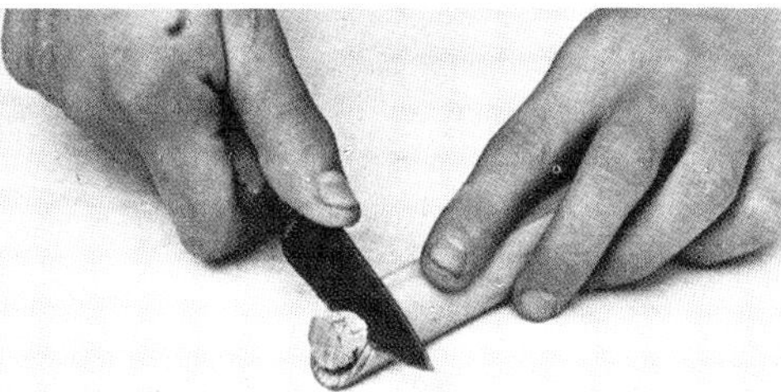

5 There should be a tiny gap at the top between the cork and the bamboo. Now try and blow a note.

A simple stringed instrument 1 Hammer a row of nails at an angle across a small wooden plank, leaving the heads sticking out.

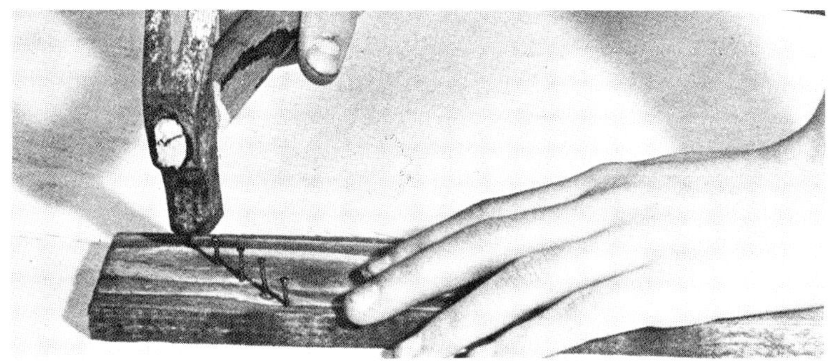

2 Put in another row of nails at the other end of the plank.

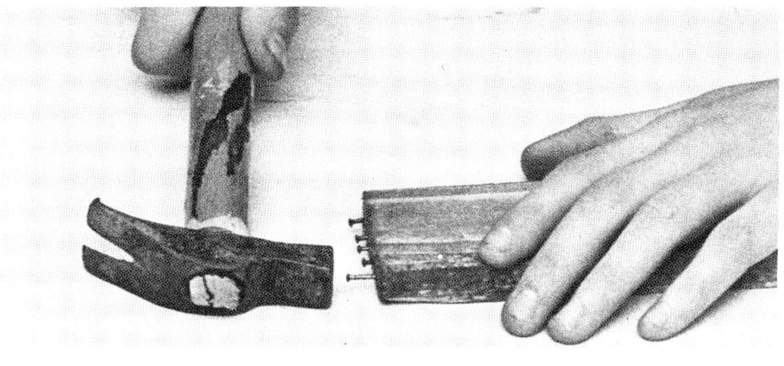

3 Tie a piece of elastic firmly onto each nail.

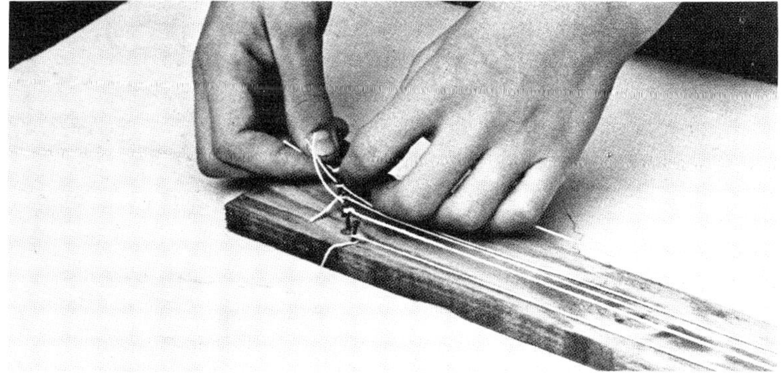

4 Pull the elastic tight and tie each string onto the nails at the other end.

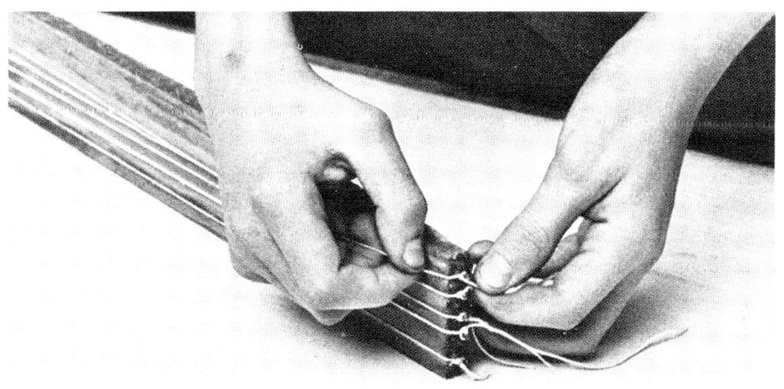

5 Push a piece of wood under the elastic so that each string is as taut as possible.

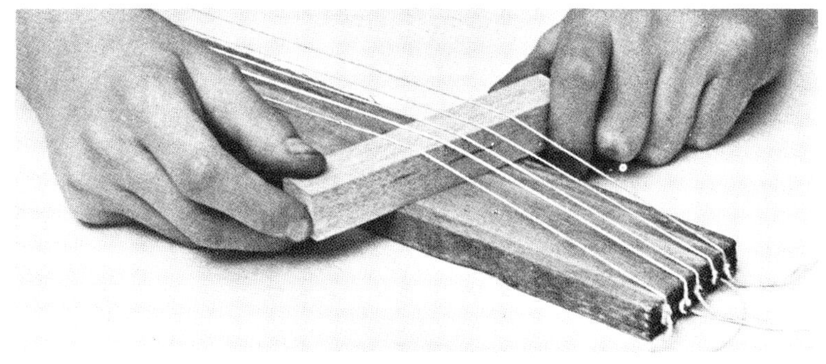

6 Now you can play a tune. Which string plays the highest note?

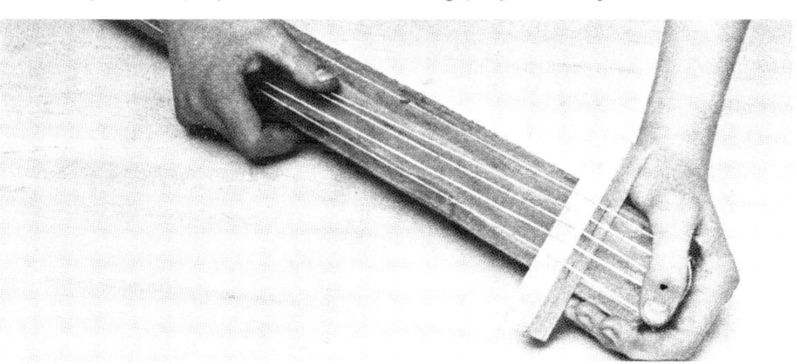

Animals and birds

1 This finch cannot reach the grubs in their holes in the bark. Rather than give up, he has collected some sharp thorns from a nearby bush and is using them as tiny spears. Man is not the only animal to have learned to use tools.

Animals use tools

Today, man has made many tools to help him; cars, aeroplanes, washing machines and sewing machines. But humans are not the only animals to have learned to use tools. All creatures use what is around them to help them find food and make a home. It is part of what we call *adaptation*. Every living thing must learn to fit in with its surroundings. Otherwise it will not survive. A finch has only a short beak, but it likes to eat the grubs living under the bark. What does it do? When faced with a challenge like this, many animals have discovered clever ways of making tools to dig holes, break open shells or pick fruit.

Even if they do not use tools, some animals learn to adapt to a new situation. Bluetits have learned to peck open milk-bottle tops to reach the cream. Some cats have even learned to take the lids off rubbish bins so that they can reach what is inside. Can you think of any more examples yourself?

2 These mangoes are growing too high up and the branches are too thin to bear his weight, so this chimp is using a stick to knock the fruit down.

3 This shellfish was too hard to crack open with his teeth, so this otter uses a stone to break it open.

1 This is a picture by Congo, the chimpanzee.

3 This is one of Congo's most famous 'abstract' pictures which was put in an exhibition.

4 Congo was three years old when he painted this picture. Do you think it looks as if it could have been done by a very small child?

2 Here you can see him painting.

Apes and monkeys

People often say that humans are descended from the apes. This is not quite true: we both share a common ancestor. Just as we have changed over the thousands of years, so have apes and monkeys. However long you try to teach an ape to talk, you will not succeed past half a dozen words or so. This is because apes simply haven't the kind of brain, or the kind of throat and tongue to make our sort of language.

That doesn't mean that they aren't intelligent. Apes, like humans, are born with few instincts but with a great ability to learn. A young ape can often be taught to operate a simple machine with as much skill as any human. Apes can be taught sign language and can 'talk' to us in this way, as well as teach it to other apes. They can even be taught to paint. Congo, at the London Zoo, had several exhibitions of his work, and many experts admired his skilful 'abstract' pictures.

5 This is the famous painting of Bacchus, the Greek god of wine, by Caravaggio, the Italian artist. It is very different from Congo's picture and yet they are both ways of painting. Which do you like best?

1 These pictures are an artist's impression of the many stages between early ape-man and man.

The arrival of man

Did our ancestors look like the monkeys and apes of today? In some ways, yes; although even six million years ago, it seems that the creature that was to become *homo sapiens sapiens* (us, in other words!) was different from early apes. All the same, we do study apes for clues about our distant past.

Apes have a complicated society and although they don't have a family life in quite the same way as we do, they make all kinds of friendships. One ape will comfort another if he is upset, by putting an arm round him. If they meet a new ape and they feel a bit frightened, they show their teeth in a snarl. Did you know that this is where *smiling* came from? We do it now as a friendly greeting!

But why, in that distant past, did we come down from the trees and walk on two feet? In the first place, early ape-man had already come a long way from the earliest little monkey-creatures, which were rather like the tree shrews we find today. Ape-man, like apes today, could see in colour, which made it easier for him to tell one thing from another. His eyes were close enough together to have what we call *stereoscopic vision*. This meant he could judge distances much better than other animals

which had eyes on either side of their heads. You can test this yourself. If you shut one eye, reach forward, and try to balance a pencil on the edge of a table, you will find that it is much harder to guess where to put it than if you use both eyes. Finally, and most important of all, man was already using his hands to pick up sticks and stones. As you can imagine, the more he used his intelligence to make tools, the more he learned, and the more his skills grew.

Then, we believe, the thick forests of Africa began to shrink, leaving more open grassland. Ape-man was ready to live on his wits and leave the safety of the trees. If he was going to make the best use of his hands, he would have to stand on two feet, not four.

Now came the time when he began to learn fast; because he had to, in order to survive in his new surroundings. Living in groups where food-gathering and defence could be shared helped him even more, especially as it meant that he could share his discoveries. Ape-man was becoming a new species – man.

1 Reindeer are perfectly adapted to living in a cold climate.

2 This tiny rat is ideally suited to living in hot desert land. Can you see how his sandy colouring blends into the background?

Animals can live everywhere

If too many animals live in the same place, eating the same food, some will not survive. So, each kind of animal must use his surroundings in a different way. They *adapt* to living differently. Squirrels and mice live in a wood - but they do not live in the same way.

How do they manage to adapt? It is a long process. An animal is born slightly different from his brothers and sisters. This difference helps him to do something that they cannot - perhaps he can run faster, jump higher, or even stay underwater longer - giving him a better chance of staying alive. He passes on to his children his own special passport for survival, and with every generation, the difference becomes more noticeable.

3 Giraffes can easily graze on the juicy leaves at the tops of trees. They can also run fast to escape their enemies.

Like us, a dolphin breathes air, because its ancestors lived on land. Yet its streamlined body is now perfectly adapted to swimming. Deer, which cannot fight their enemies, have a very sharp sense of hearing and smell to warn of danger. They can also run very fast. Even tiny fawns, scarcely an hour old, know how to run. Some creatures can hide easily because of their colouring: the fur of a brown weasel turns white in winter so that he will not show up against the snow.

Naturalists can actually guess by looking at an animal's teeth, what kind of food he eats and by looking at his coat, they can tell where he lives. Why not try this guessing game yourself?

4 Seals have beautifully streamlined bodies. They also have a layer of fat to keep them warm under their smooth shiny skin, which acts rather like a wet-suit on a diver!

1 If animals become too well adapted to their surroundings, they are in great danger when their habitats change. Giant pandas, like this one, are becoming very rare because they can only live in the bamboo forests, which are now being cut down.

2 Although whales are huge creatures, they are not dangerous and only eat the tiniest plants and animals in the sea.

Animal habits

If you look carefully, you can see how each kind of animal has adapted to its surroundings. But not only their bodies have changed to suit their way of life. Their *behaviour* alters too.

Some birds, like swallows, cuckoos and martins, fly away to a warmer country during our winter. Dormice, or bears, with no wings to escape the winter frost have another way of avoiding the cold. They *hibernate*: during the autumn, they eat as much as they can. Then they hide away, wrapping themselves up in leaves and moss and sleep until the spring sunshine wakes them up.

Perhaps animals (and this includes man!) show their most complicated and amazing behaviour when they are courting. To make the female notice him, the male puts on all kinds of displays during the mating season.

But not only do the males have to attract the females. They must also keep away the other competing males. It is a difficult and sometimes upsetting business! Most males warn off their rivals with threats, and often they have long mock-battles. In the end, it is the strongest and most cunning males that win. The losers retreat: either they will look for another female or else they must wait to see if they will be luckier next season.

1 This is a duel between two young gnus.

2 They are both fighting over a female.

3 These two male hares are competing for a female's attention. They are giving a mad acrobatic display, leaping and shadow boxing.

4 This lioness is giving her lion an affectionate nuzzle.

5 When giraffes are courting, they bleat like lambs.

1 Once upon a time there were three little pigs, who set out into the world to fend for themselves. The first thing each of them did was to build a house. Albert, the eldest, wanted a house made of straw. "Nice and airy," he said. Wilfred, the middle pig, collected sticks for his house, while Percy, the youngest, went to the brickyard for some bricks and cement.

2 Albert's straw house was soon finished, and he sat inside, happily watching his brothers at work in the hot midday sun. Before long, a wolf passed by Albert's house. "Hm," he thought. "It's a long time since I had roast pork for lunch."

The hunters and the hunted

The story of the three little pigs is just a story. But if you look at it in another way, it tells us something about the struggle between hunters and hunted.

It is a wolf's nature to eat other smaller animals, like pigs. He can do this because he has sharp teeth and claws. This wolf had the strength to knock down the two weaker houses and the intelligence to think of a way into the brick house. So the pigs could not fight him on his own ground. They had to find some other way of protecting themselves. When the three little pigs pooled their ideas, they became stronger than the wolf - although alone, they would have been an easy dinner for him.

From the very beginning, some creatures have eaten grass and plants and some - the *predators* - have eaten other, weaker animals. So one animal is always trying to outwit the another. The weaker animals and plant-eaters must watch for hungry predators, while the predators depend on other animals for *their* food.

The struggle for survival goes on every day. Only the fittest and cleverest creatures can escape their predators; while only the strongest, most cunning hunters can find enough food to stay alive.

3 "Little pig, little pig," he said, in a voice as sweet as sugar, "can I come in?" "No!" said Albert, who knew a wolf when he saw one. "Then I'll huff and I'll puff and I'll blow your house down!" said the wolf. And he blew so hard that the straw house tumbled down about Albert's ears and he only just had time to escape.

4 He ran as fast as he could to Wilfred's little wooden house. "Help!" he shouted. "Let me in!" And he bundled into the house and shut the door just as the wolf arrived.

5 "Little pigs, little pigs," said the wolf, in a voice as sweet as honey, "can I come in?" He was beginning to get really hungry and the sight of the two plump pink pigs made his mouth water. "No!" said Wilfred and Albert together. "Then I'll huff and I'll puff and I'll blow your house down!" said the wolf, licking his lips greedily.

6 "Oh dear," cried Albert. "I don't think your house is strong enough to keep out a wolf either!" And he was right. With a few huge puffs, the wolf blew the wooden house to pieces. The two little pigs ran away as fast as their trotters would carry them until they reached their youngest brother's house.

7 Percy was just laying the last brick when his brothers came panting up the path. "Quick!" shouted Albert. "The wolf!" cried Wilfred, and they all tumbled inside and barred the door. "*My* house is wolf-proof," said Percy, proudly. "It has strong brick walls and a tiled roof."

8 By now, the wolf was very hungry indeed. "Little pigs", he said, in a voice as sweet as syrup, "little pigs, can I come in?" "No!" said Percy bravely. "Then I'll huff and I'll puff and I'll blow your house down!" said the wolf. But the brick house stood firm.

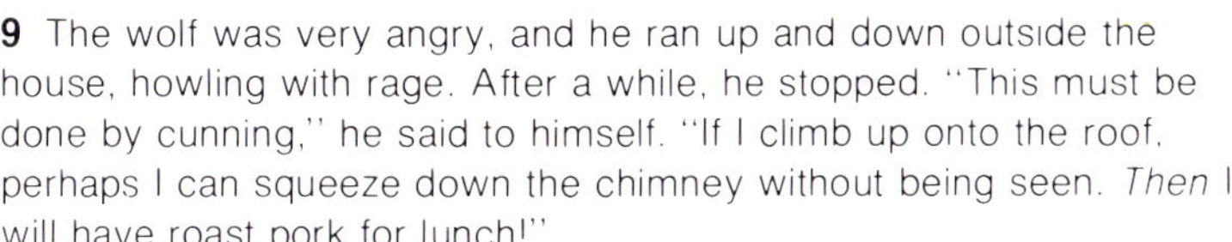

9 The wolf was very angry, and he ran up and down outside the house, howling with rage. After a while, he stopped. "This must be done by cunning," he said to himself. "If I climb up onto the roof, perhaps I can squeeze down the chimney without being seen. *Then* I will have roast pork for lunch!"

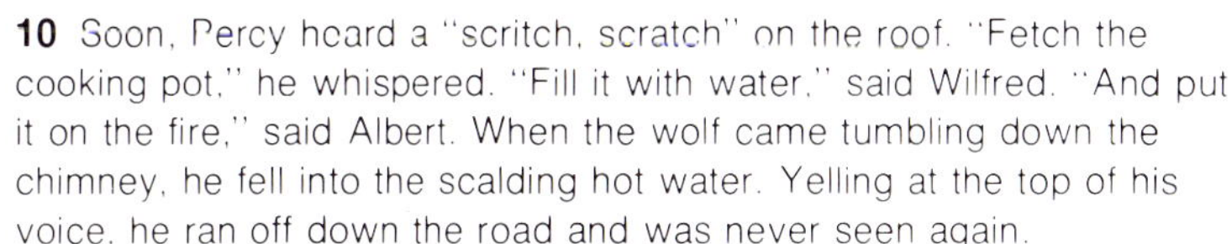

10 Soon, Percy heard a "scritch, scratch" on the roof. "Fetch the cooking pot," he whispered. "Fill it with water," said Wilfred. "And put it on the fire," said Albert. When the wolf came tumbling down the chimney, he fell into the scalding hot water. Yelling at the top of his voice, he ran off down the road and was never seen again.

1 These birds are pelicans at home in North East Africa. Some birds however migrate from as far away as this to Europe for the summer. Without compasses or any other direction-finding equipment, which our aeroplanes would need, these birds can find their way over thousands of miles.

Flying for the first time

Have you ever looked up at a flock of birds and wondered where they came from? For thousands of years, they were the only creatures that were truly masters of the air, and their story is just as interesting as ours: we believe that their ancestors were dinosaurs! It may seem odd to think that you have eaten a modern dinosaur's egg for breakfast. But it is true.

Some years ago, a man found a fossil which he *thought* was a *pterodactyl* - a flying dinosaur. But he was wrong. Another scientist saw the bones and he noticed the imprint of feathers! The very earliest bird had been discovered and it was clearly also a kind of dinosaur. All those millions of years ago, birds had found a new place to live that was safe from predators - the air.

Gradually, their bones became hollow and filled with air so that they were as light as possible. Their wings (which had once been their arms and hands) became so well adapted to flying that birds like swallows are now unable to stand on the ground at all.

To get into the air himself, man tried for a long time to copy birds. Even today, our aeroplanes are streamlined just like birds' wings. But hang-gliding is perhaps the closest we have ever come to real flying!

2 This painting by Pieter Breughel shows Daedalus, who made wings out of feathers and wax for himself and his son Icarus. When Icarus flew too near the sun, his wings melted and he fell into the sea.

3 Perhaps Daedalus really did invent the first flying apparatus that worked. Certainly, man tried for centuries to conquer the air. Even Leonardo da Vinci designed a flying machine, but he never tried it out.

4 This is a delta, a kind of hang-glider, soaring above the Mediterranean sea.

The courtship of birds

Birds, too, fight amongst themselves at mating time. Just like other animals, they spend more time threatening their rivals than fighting to kill. Some birds, however, like pheasants, can give each other a nasty slash with the sharp spurs on their feet. As soon as one male has won the battle, his unsuccessful rival will flutter off, nursing damaged feathers and wounded pride. Meanwhile, the females often appear not even to notice these terrible struggles! Once they have frightened away their rivals, the males begin their courting dance.

Some male birds have gorgeous feathers which they parade in front of the female. The bird of paradise even marks out a little 'dance floor' and tries to persuade the female to join him on it. Have you seen a peacock strutting up and down in front of the peahens, with his beautiful tail open for them to admire?

Perhaps the bower bird is the most amazing of all. When he is courting, he builds a little house for his mate out of twigs. As soon as it is ready, he decorates it inside with flowers, stones and coloured shells. Then he makes a brush out of bark and mixes up coloured earth and water to make paint which he uses to paint his house. It's a nice idea, don't you think?

1 These two golden pheasants are fighting over a female. It is a spectacular battle.

2 Kingfishers are beautiful birds that live on riverbanks, catching fish. This male kingfisher is trying to court a female by gently ruffling the feathers on her head.

3 These little birds are called long-tailed widows. The females lay their eggs in other birds' nests for them to hatch, just like cuckoos. Here you can see a male showing off his fine feathers to a female in an amazing dance.

4 A male frigate bird showing off his red pouch, which he inflates to catch the female's attention.

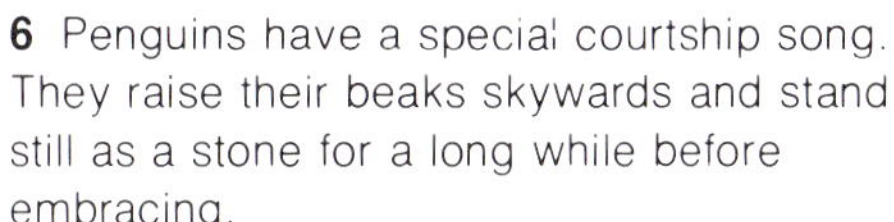

5 A frigate bird in flight with his pouch inflated.

6 Penguins have a special courtship song. They raise their beaks skywards and stand still as a stone for a long while before embracing.

The age of reptiles

1 This picture was painted by Liao, aged 11, and it is called *Lord Sè and the Palace of Dragons*. From the beginning of history we have told stories about dragons. *Were* they dinosaurs? Who knows?

2 These children have made themselves a dinosaur dragon. It has a light wooden frame which they can get inside so they can make their dragon 'walk'.

The world before mammals

Most of the animals in the world today are *mammals*. We are mammals and so are monkeys, wolves, pigs, cats and dogs. This means that we breathe air and have warm blood; we give birth to babies, not eggs, and have hair on at least some part of our bodies. But it was not always so.

As you know, animals adapt to their surroundings. Over thousands and even millions of years, they change so that they have a better chance of surviving. We call this *survival of the fittest*, because the ones best suited to their surroundings will live. Those which do not change fast enough will not have the same chance as their luckier neighbours. This changing process is called *evolution*.

It is a strange thought, but there was a time when there were hardly any mammals at all. Our ancestor-mammal was probably very small - only about five or six centimetres long; and he looked rather like a tiny mouse. He spent most of his time avoiding being eaten by the ruling creature of his day - the dinosaur. At that time, there were thousands of different kinds of dinosaurs of all sizes, just as now there are lots of different mammals. Are we then distantly descended from dinosaurs, just as we believe that birds are? No, because mammals and dinosaurs were living *at the same time*. But mammals and dinosaurs *do* share the same ancestors, which were a kind of reptile. When nearly all of our reptile-ancestors died out, the dinosaurs became the most powerful kind of creature on earth. We mammals had to wait 150 million years during the Age of Dinosaurs for our chance to come. Then, about 65 million years ago, something very strange happened. Nearly all the land creatures then living began to disappear and new kinds began to take their place. We mammals took over as the ruling kind of animals, while birds, too, spread everywhere; but the dinosaurs died out. But what *were* they like, these dinosaurs, who ruled the earth for three times as long as we mammals?

Dragons of art and legend

Everyone, whether they admit it or not, believes in monsters of one kind or another. We all know that we are unlikely to meet one; but still, most of us wonder if perhaps it *might* happen.

Some of the most famous monsters of legend have been dragons - and our pictures of dragons often look very much like some dinosaurs - except of course that dinosaurs did not breathe fire!

There are lots of legends about dragons, and one of the nicest is the story of the Lord Sè. Lord Sè loved dragons. Every part of his palace was painted with them and even his bed was carved in the shape of a sleeping dragon. One day, he woke up in his dragon-painted sheets, and looked out of his dragon-shaped windows and saw - a *real* dragon on the grass outside his palace. What did he do, this great dragon-lover? He shook like an autumn leaf and, without waiting to find out if the dragon was friendly or not, he ran out of the palace as fast as he could. No-one ever saw him again.

This is a myth, but we do have a modern dragon story - the Loch Ness Monster. Who knows whether some kind of ancient creature really does live in the deep waters of this Scottish lake?

1 This sea monster painted by Arthur Rackham is taking his friend for a ride.

2 This Dutch miniature shows the seven-headed dragon which will appear, according to ancient writings, at the end of the world.

3 The Chinese have drawn some of the most beautiful dragons, which they often see as friendly protectors – not enemies. This dragon was painted on silk many years ago by Tch'en Yong.

4 This painting by the Italian artist Uccello shows Saint George killing the dragon to save the princess.

Once upon a dinosaur

Dinosaurs may have died out a long time ago, but we still think about them today. Perhaps because we don't need to be afraid of them any longer, we often make them out to be friendly creatures, no more terrible than a large elephant. Some of them, of course, were not so terrifying; but others, like Tyrannosaurus Rex, must have been more dangerous than any living creature today.

Here you can see how we believe a real dinosaur must have looked, together with some cartoons which look at him rather more disrespectfully.

Making a dinosaur

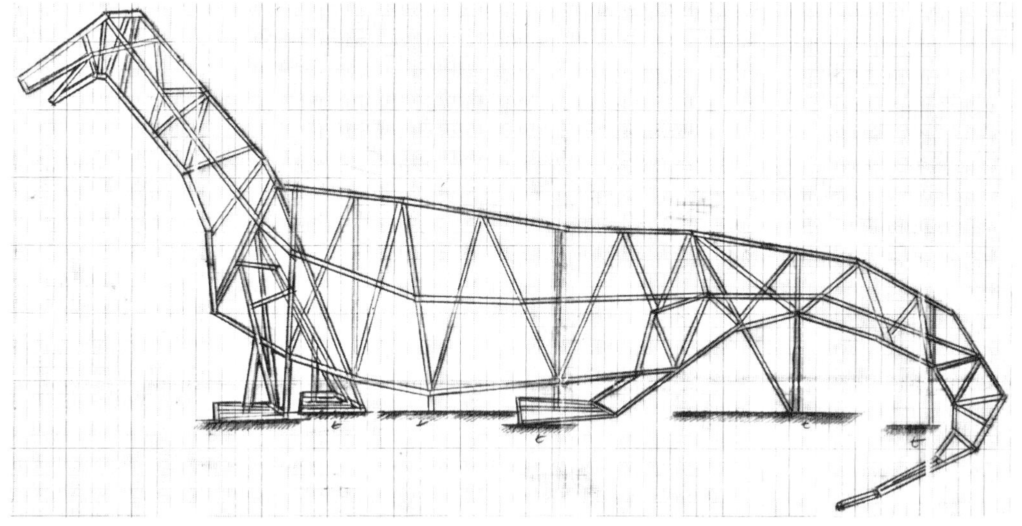

1 This model of a dinosaur was designed by an artist who helped these children to build it themselves. The dinosaur is 6 metres long.

2 Here, a boy is nailing two pieces of the skeleton together.

3 These bits of wood are too long, so this boy is sawing them off.

4 Here, the whole frame is laid out on the floor.

These children were so interested in dinosaurs that they wanted to see one. But there are no real dinosaurs left today. All we can see now are fossilized bones in museums and pictures in books of how we *think* they must have looked.

"Let's build a dinosaur of our own," suggested Caroline. "But dinosaurs are much too big," said Stephen. "It wouldn't fit into our classroom." "Then we will make a baby dinosaur," decided the rest of the class. Even so, their dinosaur was going to be about six metres long. There are lots of different kinds of dinosaur they could have chosen; but here you can see the one they made, with the help of their teacher.

First of all, they drew a plan. Then they made the skeleton out of strips of plywood which they laid out on the floor and nailed together. To make the skin, they first covered the skeleton with sheets of newspaper. They needed lots of layers so that their dinosaur would not look too boney. Then they painted him red and green and brown.

If you made a dinosaur, it would probably look very different from theirs. Why don't you ask an adult to help you build one of your own? You could make a very tiny one, if you wanted, that would fit on top of a table, or even in a matchbox.

5 Now the dinosaur begins to take shape. These children are lifting up his backbone.

6 Now they add his ribs, joining the back to the underside.

7 This must be done carefully, or the dinosaur will be crooked.

8 Next, the skeleton is neatly finished off.

9 Now, they begin to make his head.

10 These children are building a long tail.

11 Now they have joined everything together and added the feet, and it begins to look like a dinosaur. All it needs is a skin.

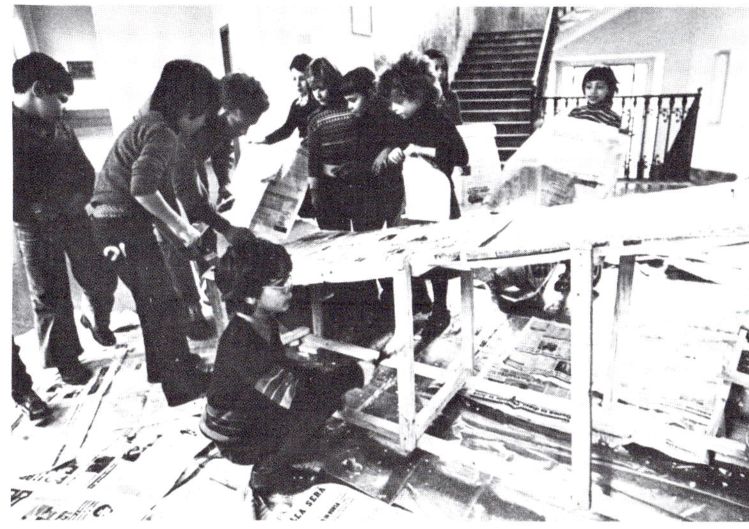

12 For the skin, they begin covering the skeleton with sheets of newspaper.

13 It takes quite a while to cover the dinosaur's body.

14 Now they have reached the head.

15 The head is a difficult shape to cover.

16 Finally, they cover the tail.

17 First, they paint the skin all over with thick, white paint.

18 Here you can see the finished dinosaur. The children have painted him all over with dinosaur colours.

1 This dinosaur, painted by a group of 9-year-old Italian children, is so huge that the palm trees hardly come up to his knees.

2 This dinosaur, painted by 9-year-old Lucy, looks rather like a tortoise

Dinosaur drawings

No-one knows exactly what dinosaurs looked like. This is because it is very rare indeed to discover a complete fossilized skeleton. Usually we find just a bone or two - sometimes only a few teeth. Often, too, there are bones from many other animals mixed together. How can anyone unravel such a difficult jigsaw - especially as many of the vital pieces are missing? Even when experts have put a skeleton together, they still do not have a complete picture of the dinosaur. Think of an elephant: if you only saw his bones, would you guess that he had a trunk?

Why don't you try to draw a dinosaur yourself? It could be a dangerous, meat-eating monster from a primeval swamp; or even a funny cartoon animal.

3 John, aged 10, painted a baby dinosaur lost in the wilderness.

4 Nick and Maddy, both aged 9, painted a dinosaur with horns, a *triceratops*. ▶

5 This is a family of dinosaurs, painted by Sally and Rachel, both aged 10.

6 Rupert, aged 10, painted this dinosaur in a meadow.

7 Junko, aged 7, painted her dinosaur all yellow.

8 Gareth, aged 11, painted two different kinds of dinosaur, a *brontosaurus* and a *stegosaurus*.

9 These two little dinosaurs have only just hatched from their eggs and they were painted by 10-year-old Marianne.

10 Winsome, aged 9, painted five dinosaurs which live in a lake.

The age of dinosaurs

What was the dinosaur's world like? In those days, most of the earth was much hotter and wetter and looked rather like the tropical forests and swamps today. There were gigantic ferns and evergreens, very similar to our modern conifers, and there were also trees rather like palms. There were no seasons and all the year round it was summer.

Dinosaurs were a kind of reptile, and reptiles had made a big advance on the earlier amphibians. (These were creatures like modern frogs, that lived partly on land, partly in the water, where they laid their eggs.) Reptiles could lay eggs with tough shells. This meant that they did *not* have to live near water all the time. They could move around on dry land. Their eggs were much safer, because they could bury them in warm sand or mud to hatch out in the sun. The dinosaurs passed this advantage on to their distant descendants, the birds.

On the right of the picture is *Archaeopterix*, the first bird. He was different from *Pterodactyls*, or flying dinosaurs, which glided rather than flew, and had no feathers. *Archaeopterix* had a wishbone, proving that he was a *real* bird. He is one of the most important fossils ever found, because although he is clearly a bird, he is also clearly a dinosaur! This means that we can actually see evolution working. We can see the changeover from one kind of creature to another.

Some of the plant-eating dinosaurs were immense. *Diplodocus* (you can see him in the picture) was about 30 metres long - about the length of three double-decker buses in a row! It is something of a mystery how his tiny mouth managed to feed such a vast body. There was *Stegosaurus*, built like a tank. He had huge plates down his back and spikes on his tail to fight off predators. (You can see him on the hill in the picture.) Then there was *Tyrannosaurus Rex*, perhaps the most ferocious creature ever to have lived. He ate meat and his huge, pointed teeth were like steak knives. He was nearly 15 metres long - about the size of a tennis court.

The dinosaurs have left us with many mysteries, but maybe the greatest is the reason why they died out. Perhaps it was because the climate became much colder. More important still, the earth began to have seasons. We know this because the first trees to drop their leaves in winter began to appear. For several months each year there would have been no food for the plant-eating dinosaurs; and when *they* died, their predators would have starved too.

So the dinosaurs disappeared, giving the mammals their great chance. They took it; and they had two big advantages: they could stay warm in winter and, most important of all, they gave birth to babies which they cared for themselves. They could make sure that the next generation would survive.

1 This is a snake charmer with two deadly cobras. Snakes have a very poor sense of hearing, so perhaps it is the sight of the charmer's moving fingers that has hypnotized them.

2 This beautiful snake is called a coral snake and it has a deadly bite. Like many dangerous creatures, it is banded red, yellow and black. Another snake, the scarlet king snake, looks very similar but is harmless. It is protected because it has the 'danger' markings.

3 A few other reptiles also have a poisonous bite, like this Mexican beaded lizard.

Poisonous reptiles

Snakes were amongst the last reptiles to appear. The biggest kinds, like pythons, are strong enough to catch their prey by squeezing it to death. Others have another way of protecting themselves. They are poisonous. Their poison glands are rather like the ones that make saliva in our own mouths. These glands are next to their sharp fangs, so that when a snake bites someone, the poison runs into the cut. But not all snakes are poisonous - many are quite harmless.

Some of the most dangerous snakes have brightly coloured bands of red, yellow or black, as if to advertise their powers. Think of a wasp or a hornet. It is almost as if these bands are a natural warning system. Some quite harmless creatures, however, have markings like their more deadly relatives as a protection against predators.

1 This is an African crocodile: it looks really prehistoric with its thick-plated skin and rows of pointed teeth. And so he is. He has remained almost unchanged from the Age of the Dinosaurs.

2 These turtles are also living fossils. They do no harm to anyone and often live to a great age. Today, some kinds are in danger of dying out, because they have been killed in their thousands by man.

Reptiles

Many kinds of reptiles have died out since the Age of Dinosaurs. Today, luckily for us, they are smaller than they once were, but they still lay eggs like their primitive ancestors.

All animals need heat to move about quickly. Mammals' bodies stay at the same temperature all the time, so they have energy even in cold weather. But reptiles depend on the warmth of their surroundings to give them the heat they need. That is why you will see lizards or snakes basking in the sunshine. In winter, many of them hide away in holes where they lie, hardly moving, until spring.

Some reptiles have remained almost unchanged for millions of years. We call these *living fossils*. Some, like turtles, have been recorded as living up to two hundred years old. Perhaps it is because they live such unhurried lives!

3 This is a trial of strength between two male green lizards. Lizards, like crocodiles and turtles, are reptiles.

1 Animals were only able to leave the water and live on land because plants were already growing there. Today, a great oak tree like this can give food and shelter to thousands of creatures, large and small.

2 Plants like these lichens can live even on cold, wind-swept mountain-sides.

3 Fungi are also a kind of plant, although they get their food from the remains of other living things, like old tree trunks and dead leaves.

Plants made life possible

The story of the earth is not complete without the plants. Did you know that without plants, there could have been no other life at all?

Each plant is an amazingly complex factory. It turns sunlight into food, which it uses to grow. As it does this, it gives off oxygen. In this way, the air we breathe is made by plants. It has been proved that before plants lived on earth, there was no oxygen in the air.

Plants first began in the sea. Even today, although it is hard to believe, more kinds live in the sea than on land. They fed the early sea creatures, just as they now feed millions of fish. But slowly, all those years ago, some of these sea plants grew a tough skin. This meant that when they came out of the water, they would not dry out. Little by little, these new plants spread on land. Looking for food, sea creatures followed the plants. If there had been no plants for food and shelter, no creature (or even insect) could have lived on land.

Towards the end of the Age of Dinosaurs, a new kind of plant began growing. It was a flowering plant; and since then, nearly all our land plants have flowers of some kind.

4 This plant is a kind of cactus. It stores water in its thick leaves and can live in very dry places.

5 Here is a field full of buttercups. See how they open up their petals to the sunshine.

Life began in water

1 This modern amphibian is a tree frog, and it eats insects. Its green colouring means that it can live safely among the leaves, and it can jump like an acrobat.

2 Frogs must lay their soft, jelly-like eggs in water. Eggs without a tough shell make an easy meal for a hungry predator.

3 Here you can see the tiny tadpoles developing inside their eggs.

Animals with a double life

The plants left the sea for the as yet unexplored land. But not long after this, some fish, too, were preparing to make an extraordinary change in their way of life. They were developing lungs, so that they could breathe out of the water; and they were growing stubby legs which would carry them about on dry land. We suppose that this change came about because the fish which did manage to reach land found that there were many plants to eat and no predators. It was clearly a good place to be!

But '*amphibian*' is Greek for 'double life'. These early creatures (and modern amphibians) could not move far from the sea. They had to spend at least half of their lives in water.

4 The tadpoles have broken out of their eggs, but they must still live in water.

5 This tadpole has developed legs. It is becoming a frog.

6 It is almost as if evolution has to take place all over again in the life of each amphibian! Now the tail has nearly disappeared.

1 This is one of man's most successful swimming machines – *Nautilus*, the American nuclear submarine. But unlike a fish, it still has to come to the surface for fresh supplies of food and air.

2 These fish are beautifully suited to their surroundings. They can sense the slightest disturbance in the water which will signal either food or the approach of an enemy.

Fish

Amphibians were the first fish to come out of the water and after millions of years, one of their kind developed into a reptile. Time passed and one of these reptile species at last evolved into the first mammal. It has been a long process, and there are still many, many questions which no-one can answer. *Which* reptile; *which* amphibian, *which* fish? And why? We can still only guess although we do have clues which prove that this is really what happened.

Did you know that for a few days, every mammal, and this includes man, has a tail while it is developing inside its mother? Scientists believe it is a strange reminder of our ancient ancestors who lived in the sea.

3 A shark is one of the most ancient kinds of fish, but submarines have 'copied' their perfectly streamlined shape.

But only a few kinds of fish came out of the sea. Many of them were so well suited to their surroundings that they stayed where they were, becoming even better adapted to their watery life. Fish are now perfect swimming machines: they can breathe, find food and escape their enemies. Everything they need is in the water, so why should they leave it?

Some fish, like sharks, have changed only a little over the millions of years. A few years ago, fishermen off East Africa were surprised to catch a *coelacanth*, a fish which was supposed to have died out over 65 million years ago!

4 These fish are called kissing gourami. The sea creatures have just as complicated patterns of behaviour underwater as animals do on land, and we have only recently begun to learn about them.

1 Some creatures today, like these water fleas still hide on the bottom of shallow pools, like their distant ancestors, the trilobites.

2 Other early sea creatures looked like strange and beautiful flowers. They learned to fix themselves to the sea floor, like this sea worm today, which trails its tentacles in the water, waiting for a meal to drift its way.

The first creatures of all

Before fish ever appeared on the bottom of the shallow seas, other forms of life had been developing quietly in the warm primeval waters for millions of years.

It is amazing to think that some sea creatures today are very similar to their ancestors. They were there before the dinosaurs, before human beings came down from the trees, and yet their kind have still survived.

The earliest creatures to leave a real fossil record of how they looked were the first ones to build up a hard shell. We suppose that they did this as protection against being eaten - or maybe against being hurt by rocks or sea.

Amongst these first shellfish were the *trilobites*. They were the ancestors of our modern shrimps and lobsters, and they lived on the bottom of shallow sunny water. At that time, no living things had explored the land or the deeper oceans.

There was certainly another sort of living creature in those primeval seas, but they were probably as tiny then as they are today. We call their modern relatives *plankton*. These creatures are carried along by the current and they can travel in this way for thousands of miles. If you looked at a bottle filled with the sea water where they were living, you would only be able to see hundreds of tiny moving dots.

Plankton are eaten by the larger animals in the sea today, just as they were all those millions of years ago. But some of the very earliest floating creatures are not minute - the jellyfish. They did not build up a hard shell, perhaps because they had a sting instead.

There is a third kind of early sea creature. They look very much like beautiful plants, because they fix themselves to rocks or the sandy sea bottom; but they are in fact animals. Sea lilies, which trailed their long arms in the current, patiently waiting for a meal of plankton to drift their way, are now extinct: but sea anemones, sponges and beautiful, coloured corals still have many descendants today.

The last kind of creature to develop in the sea were the swimmers; and they were the first to have bones. To begin with, these early fish crept along the warm, sandy sea bottom, dredging up plants and tiny animals with open mouths like small scoops. But over millions of years they became more adventurous. They learned to swim farther afield. Today, many fish have blue-grey backs which blend in with the blue water, so they are difficult to see from above. Often, they have pale underbellies because if you are underwater, looking *upwards*, the surface of the water seems white-coloured. Try it and see, with a pair of goggles!

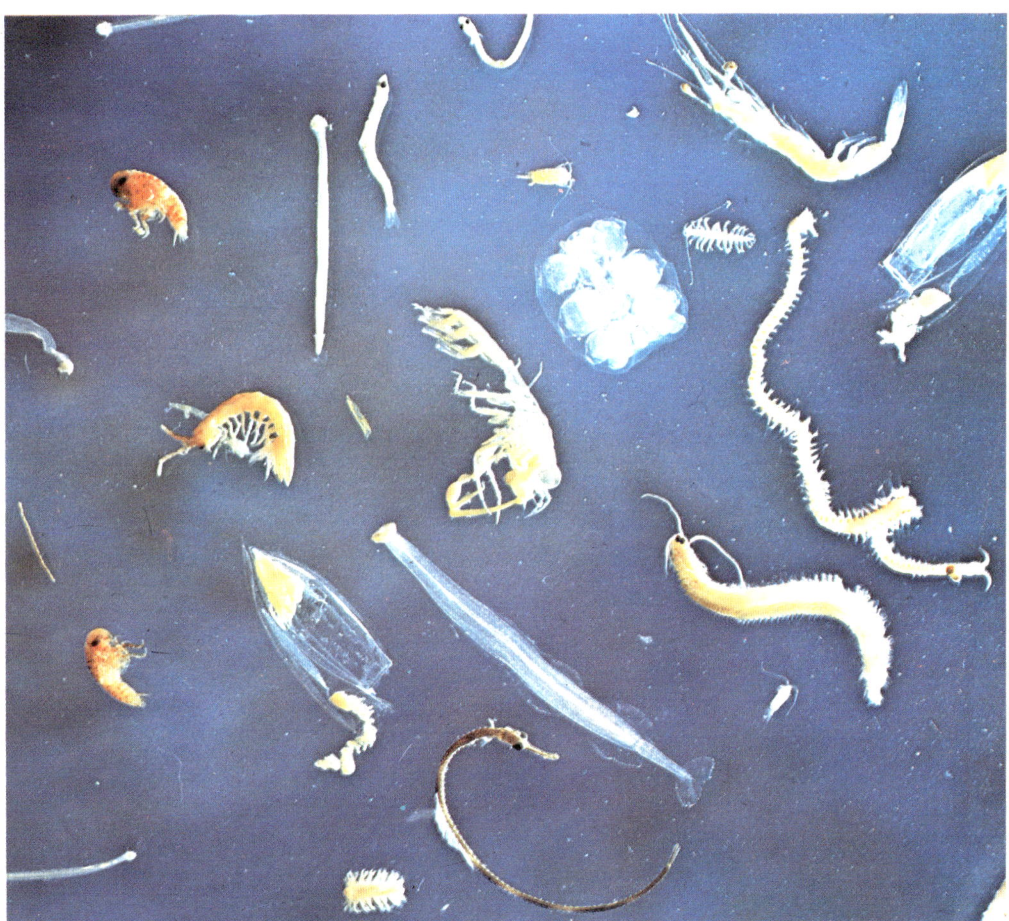

3 These are *plankton*, magnified many times. They are really thousands of different kinds of tiny creatures and plants, floating about in the current.

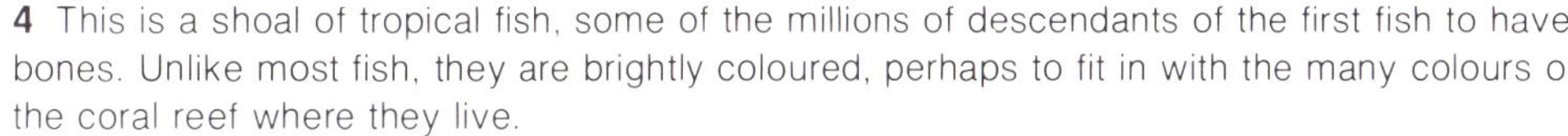

4 This is a shoal of tropical fish, some of the millions of descendants of the first fish to have bones. Unlike most fish, they are brightly coloured, perhaps to fit in with the many colours of the coral reef where they live.

1 Life first began on the still, warm waters of the shallow ancient seas.

How life began

But what happened before the jellyfish, the trilobites and the plankton, these first creatures that lived in the ancient seas? How did life on earth begin?

Before the animals there were primitive plants called *algae*. They didn't have leaves, and they didn't have flowers; they probably looked like a slimy green smear on the rocks. But for nearly one half of its 4,600 million-year-long history, there had been no life at all on earth. Now, the whole chain of evolution was about to begin.

But what happened before the plants? This is perhaps the most amazing part of the whole story. We think that, at that time, the world looked nothing like it does today. For millions of years, the surface of the earth was bare rock, without soil or sand, swept by violent, hot winds. Tropical rain beat down upon the seas, and we can still see the ripple

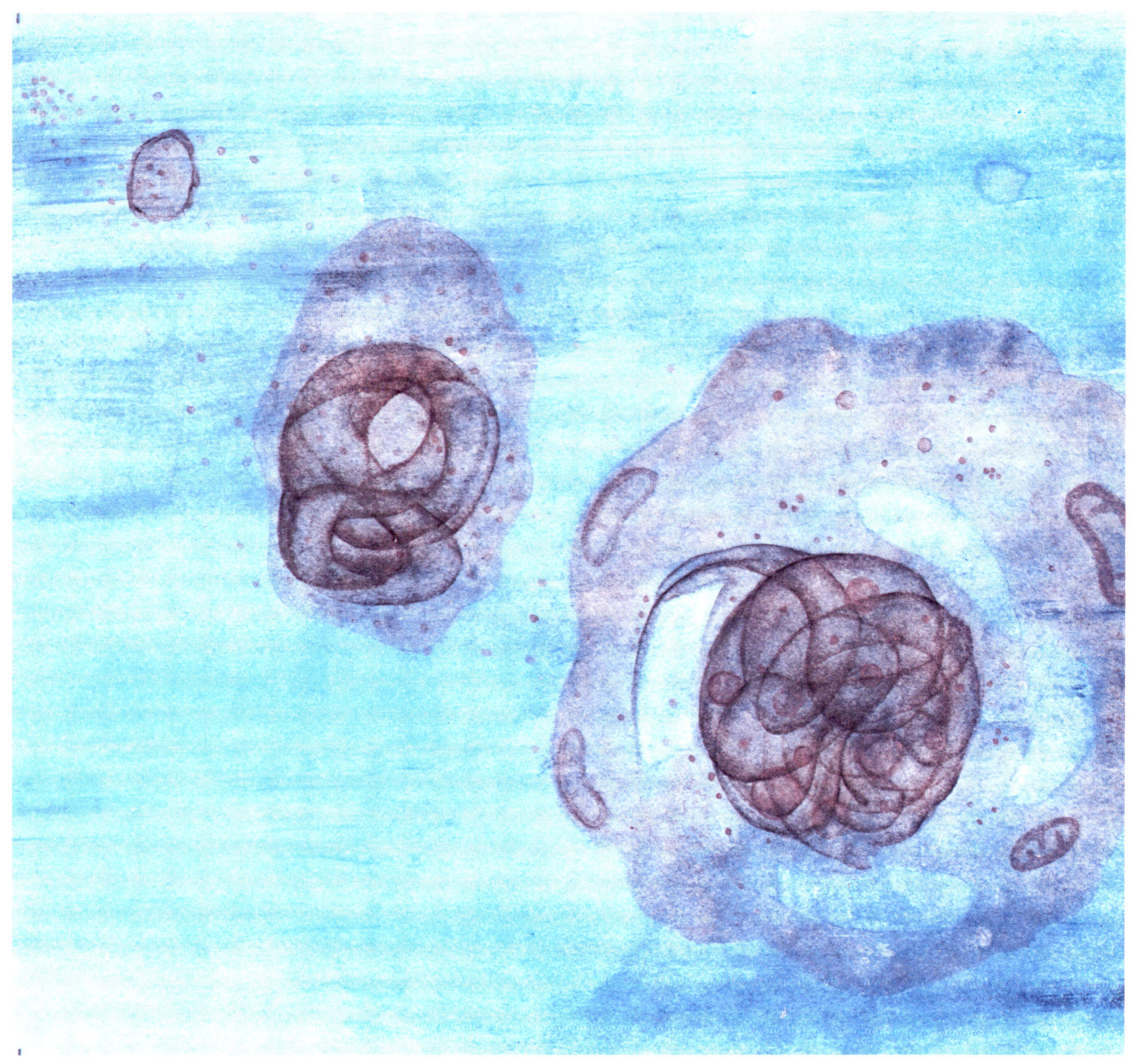

2 Millions and millions of years ago, from the *organic soup* created in the seas, the first cells of living creatures developed. We still do not know exactly how.

marks of these ancient oceans in the oldest rocks and the pattern of rain drops from rainstorms long past. Nothing lived on earth; but there was water and certain materials which we are coming to believe are the building blocks of life: *methane*, *ammonia* and *hydrogen*. In the warm, still waters around the shores, these combined to form *organic* material – the material which makes up living things. Scientists have tried to re-create these conditions in their laboratories, and they, too, have made this *organic soup*, as they call it. But still, the largest question of all is yet to be answered. How did these organic materials, shapeless and not yet alive, come to arrange themselves in the complicated, highly organised way that was necessary if they were to become cells of plants and animals? How did they become living things?

The Ice Age

1 This is a great glacier in Greenland. Once, a huge ice sheet stretched as far as England. It gouged out great valleys and sheared off mountain peaks. We can still see its work today in the mountains of Scotland.

How ice changed the earth

The earth we see today is nothing like the earth our ancestors saw, while if we could travel back to the time when life was first beginning, we would not believe we were on the same planet. Rocks which were on the surface of the earth are now many miles under its crust, the seas are in different places and even the weather is not the same. This is due to the great changes that have happened both inside and outside our planet.

One of the changing forces was ice! At certain times, the ice caps at either the North, or the South poles, have spread and spread until they covered thousands of miles. In the last great Ice Age, the ice sheet reached to just north of London!

The earth is a spinning ball in space, going round the sun. Scientists believe that from time to time it changes the way it spins very, very slightly, and this is enough to change the weather completely. If it gets colder the winters become longer. The snow does not melt from one year to the next and so, over hundreds of years, the land is covered by a thick sheet of solid ice. This ice presses down on the hills and mountains, scraping away solid rock and gouging out U-shaped valleys; splitting off huge boulders and carrying them hundreds of miles in frozen rivers, or *glaciers.*

What do we see today? In places like Wales and Scotland, you can clearly see how the ice has carved the ranges of hills into smooth, rounded shapes. They are not nearly as high and craggy as they were before the Ice Age.

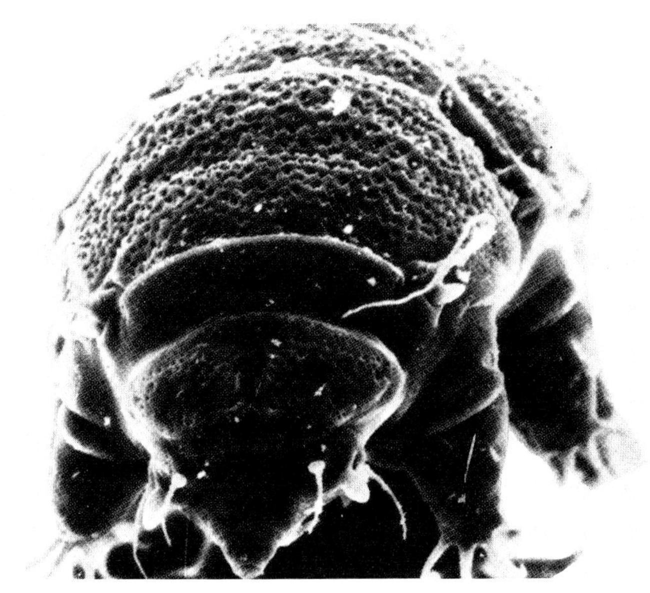

2 Many animals fled the cold. Only a few, which managed to adapt to the ice, like this tiny tardigrade, managed to survive.

When will we have another Ice Age? It is difficult to tell: some experts say that we are approaching one at the moment. But whether this is true or not, it will take thousands of years before we actually see it happening.

Today, in the highest and coldest mountain ranges like the Alps and the Himalayas, the ice never melts. Great glaciers slide slowly down these mountains, sometimes only a few metres a year, until they reach lower, warmer land where they melt. Looking at them now we can imagine what it must have been like when Scotland looked like Antarctica and whole countries were buried under the ice.

1 How does ice "carry" objects? You can test this for yourself. Put a heavy iron wire on a block of ice.

2 Although the ice is still solid, it will melt where the wire has been placed, so that it sinks into it.

3 The block re-freezes over the top of the wire, which continues on down through the ice.

1 Not all animals were forced to move. This family of tree sloths has lived in South America for millions of years.

2 This anteater also, has always lived in South America.

The time of change

What happened to the animals during the Ice Ages? Compared to the huge time scales of the history of the earth, the last Ice Age was very recent indeed. It was about 18,000 years ago, when early man already knew how to use tools and hunt animals.

Some animals like the hairy mammoth, and the sabre toothed tiger and the bison, were able to adapt to the fierce cold and they grew thick warm coats. Those which could not change died out, or fled to warmer countries.

3 This scaley tree pangolin also eats insects. It comes from South Africa.

4 This is an armadillo distantly related to pangolins and anteaters. It now lives in both North and South America.

A dressing-up costume 1 Cut a piece of hessian about one metre wide and one and a half metres long.

2 Fold the edges to the middle, as you can see here.

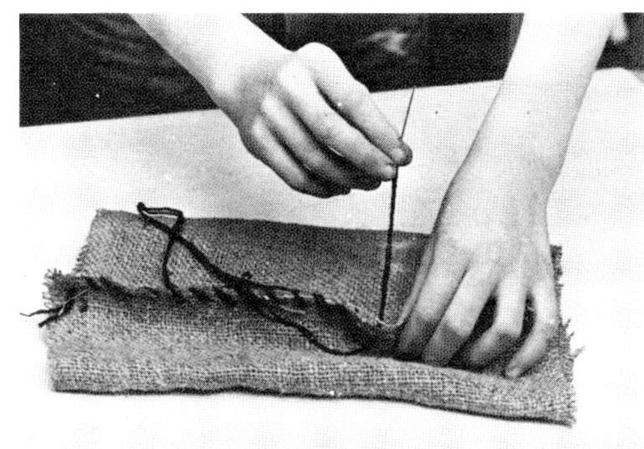

3 Sew the edges together, but leave a few cms open for the neck opening.

Man in the Ice Age

What happened to man, when the ice sheets stretched down from the North Pole? He was luckier than many of the animals because he had already discovered fire. He learned to shelter in caves and to skin animals for their fur to make warm clothes and rugs to sleep on.

Because of the ice, the northern seas were much lower than they had been, and the Bering Straits between Asia and North America was probably almost a land bridge. Animals like the sabre-toothed tiger, bears, deer and bison had already crossed from one continent to another, and soon, the ancestors of the North American Indians began the long, cold journey from Asia to their new home.

Today we do not need to skin wild animals for our clothes; but you might like to try to make this simple stone age coat. Perhaps our ancestors wore something a little like this to keep out the Ice-Age damp and cold!

4 Cut holes for your arms, but make sure the holes are big enough.

5

6

7

5 For the hood, fold another rectangular piece of hessian in two and sew up one side.

6 Sew the hood on round the neck opening.

7 Sew up the shoulder seams and your costume is ready.

8 Stone age children may have worn clothes a little like this: and some nomadic herdsmen still do!

8

After the Ice Age

Nearly every country in the world has a myth about a great flood which drowned everyone, except for a few chosen people and animals who were saved to begin a new world.

We can now try to imagine what it must have been like for early man after the last Ice Age, for when the ice melted, there must have been tremendous floods. Although the great cold and the melting did not happen suddenly but over hundreds of years, it must still have been a time of great change for our ancestors. Perhaps - and we do not know - this was the time we are remembering in these ancient legends.

How Yima saved the world

The ancient Persians wrote the history of their world in a book called the *Zend Avesta*, which tells of the history of their world. It tells how Ahura Mazda, God of the world spoke to Yima and said, "Yima I have chosen you, because you are a wise and brave man, not like your neighbours who have angered me greatly. Soon, dark clouds will form and snow will fall on the evil earth. Until this day, I have made the fields full of green growing plants, watered by soft rains and warmed by our sun. But from this day, snow will cover everything. So, Yima, to escape death in the great cold, you must build a huge cavern under the earth. It will be as long and wide as the distance a horse can gallop. In this shelter, you must gather together the seed of those men and women you find most beautiful, the swiftest birds in the air, the strongest and best tempered of your flocks and herds and the loveliest and most useful creatures in the world. Then you must gather the seed of your best-loved plants, trees and a measure of corn, and coals of red burning fire."

Then the Wise One continued, "Your shelter must be built in this way. At the top, there shall be five passages, in the middle six and at the bottom, three. In the top-most passages you must put one thousand men and one thousand women, in the middle

six hundred and at the bottom, three hundred. Then you must make a door, so that light can reach even the dark corners of the shelter."

Yima obeyed Ahura Mazda, and built the shelter as he had been instructed. As the Wise One had foretold, the snow fell and the world became one white desert. Every living creature died of the cold. But at the end of that long, long winter, Yima opened the shelter and the people and all the creatures, birds, trees and flowers he had collected went out on the earth, and it was no longer empty.

How the Indians escaped the flood

The Amazon Indians have their own story of a great flood. One day, a hunting party met an old man whose name was Arunderi, and he said to them, "Take all your canoes and paddle up stream as far as you can. Then climb up to the very top of the highest mountain, because soon, every river will break its banks and there will be a great flood."

The Indians hurried away, and no sooner were they safely on the highest mountain peak, than the rains began to fall.

Before long, the whole country was covered with water, and the Indians watched anxiously as the water rose up the mountain. Suddenly, out of the falling rain came a huge fish. Walking on his fins, he climbed right to where the Indians were huddled and he took all their children into his mouth. Then he swam away with them through the water; and from that moment, the rain stopped. Then came a turtle and the chief of the Indians said, "Turtle, dive down through the water and see if you can find land." But however deep he dived, the turtle could not reach the bottom. "Try once more," said the chief, and the turtle dived one last time.

He did not reach the bottom, but he did find a leaf, still growing underwater on a tree. Then the chief knew that the waters were slowly sinking. Soon all the Indians were able to come down from the mountain and there they found their children waiting. The fish had carried them to safety.

1 A photographer shows the changing season in a favourite place in the Dolomites. Here, it is January and the snow lies thick on the ground.

4 April: sometimes, winter has one last surprise for these mountain regions. Just as spring has come, there is another sprinkling of snow.

The changing seasons

Today in England, as in many countries of the world, we take the seasons for granted. Summer follows spring, winter follows autumn, and we look forward to each changing time of the year for something different - whether it is strawberries or snowballs. But now we believe it was not always like this. Once, in the time of the dinosaurs, there was little difference between winter and summer - it was always hot and steamy and tropical. Then we believe that the weather changed. It grew cooler, and

2 February: the thaw is just beginning. Snow melts uncovering the brown earth.

3 March: winter is nearly over, and the grass is beginning to look green again although snow still lies on the mountain.

5 May: spring has really arrived and the meadow is thick with buttercups and daisies.

6 The sun is hot in June and the air seems almost misty with the smell of meadow sweet and warm grass. There is still snow on the high rocks.

7 It is July, and the grass is dark, rich green.

10 October: the grass is yellow and the pine woods are looking browner.

although parts of the world were still hot and wet, the ice caps grew at the North and South Pole, and for the first time, we began to have a sharp difference between summer and winter. This was the time when the mammals first began to live everywhere on earth, and when man, who is good at adjusting to change, began to put his special talents to the test.

Most people like having seasons, because there is always something new to see. Why don't you do what this photographer in the Dolomites has done. He has carefully watched one favourite place through each season to see how it changes.

8 In August it often rains in the mountains and you can hardly see the mountains for mist. See how the colours have changed.

9 September is calm and clear. You can tell there is a sharpness in the air and the cloud shadows pass over the mountains.

11 With November comes the first snow, speckling the meadow and low clouds are tangled in the fir trees.

12 December: the snow lies thick and even the sky is a flat white colour. The countryside waits for spring.

The shaping of land and sea

Volcanoes are often responsible for warm mineral springs, such as those in Iceland or New Zealand. Minerals from the earth dissolve in the warm waters and they are often used in health cures. This cascade in Ethiopia is made of mineral salts which have been left after the waters have dried up.

◀ **1** This is the beginning of a volcanic eruption. First, the mountain begins to smoke.

2 Then a cloud of gas bursts out, followed by burning sparks and rocks. ▶

When the earth was a ball of fire

But what happened before life on earth? How did the world come to look as it does now? These are questions that scientists think they may now be able to answer.

In the beginning, we believe that the earth was much bigger than it is now. It was boiling hot and made of molten rock and gases. Slowly it began to cool and as it cooled it shrank, although the surface was still seething like a cauldron, and covered with volcanoes, blasting out fiery molten rock, gas and steam. Eventually, it cooled enough for the steam to turn to water, and a crust formed on the earth like a skin of ice on a puddle. Even today, this crust is only 5-25 miles thick! Underneath, the earth is boiling hot and moving, like a vast pot of thick soup. Another strange fact we now know, is that the crust is broken up into huge *plates*, like pieces of a gigantic jigsaw which grind up against each other, floating on the *mantle* as the interior of the earth is called.

Each plate covers many millions of square miles. So you can imagine, where they are bumping into each other, there are huge stresses and strains. This is where we have earthquakes and volcanoes. We cannot *see* the cracks between the plates because they have become silted up with layers of rock, rather in the way that a mass of driftwood is bound together with weed and twigs. All the same, we can draw a very rough map of where we believe them to be, by following the chains of volcanoes and the earthquake patterns all over the earth.

How is a volcano formed? Where two plates meet, the pressure is so great that one is pushed very slightly under the other. This means that some of the earth's crust is pressed into the boiling hot mantle underneath. It melts; and when enough has

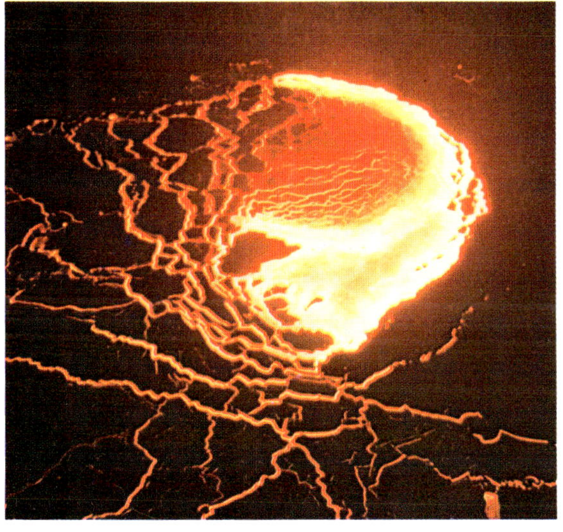

◀ **3** Soon, a mass of molten lava boils up to the mouth of the crater.

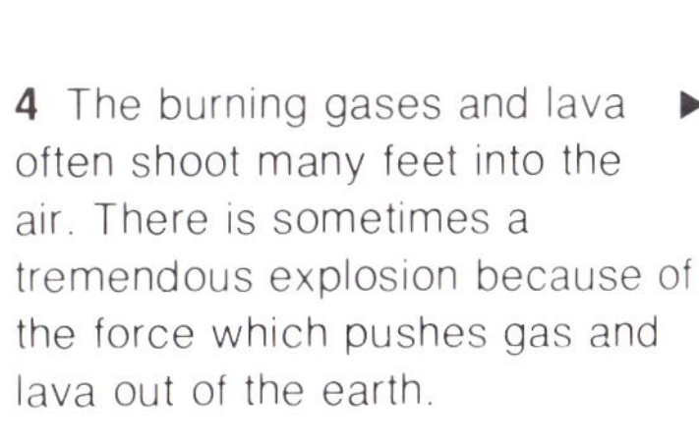

4 The burning gases and lava often shoot many feet into the air. There is sometimes a tremendous explosion because of the force which pushes gas and lava out of the earth. ▶

5 Now the lava begins pouring down the mountain, sometimes as fast as 200 km an hour!

6 Molten rock is spilling out from all parts of the crater and shooting down the rocks in hundreds of brilliant rivers of fire.

collected, it forces its way up through the crust like steam spurting out of a kettle. And it can happen very suddenly. One afternoon a Mexican farmer noticed a small hollow in one of his fields. He was puzzled because he hadn't seen it before, but he filled it in with earth. Some while later, just after 4 o'clock on 20th February 1943, a huge, gaping pit appeared, bubbling grey ash. Twenty four hours later, the cone of a volcano, 50 metres high, was thrusting through the ground, and spilling out boiling lava. A few months later, there was a new mountain, 500 metres high, which had swallowed up all the surrounding villages.

It is hard to imagine temperatures so hot, that rocks will melt; but that is the kind of furnace that is a volcano. When it erupts, temperatures of about 2,100°C have been measured which is twenty times the boiling point of water! In 1815, a volcano in Indonesia called Tambora erupted and we guess now that the explosion was about equal to 16,000 megatons. The A-bomb at Hiroshima at the end of the Second World War was only 0.02 megatons!

When molten rock shoots out of the volcano as *lava*, it soon cools and becomes solid; but it has become a special kind of rock. We call it *igneous* rock, because it has been made by heat, and *ignis* is the Latin word for fire.

Precious stones like rubies, beryls, topazes, olivines, and even diamonds are made by volcanoes. We find the rough gem stones, like little bits of nut, in the chocolate of the surrounding igneous rock.

If we trace the igneous rocks, we can guess where volcanoes have been. We know that millions of years ago, there were huge volcanoes in Scotland. Edinburgh castle is built on what is left of an immense, extinct volcano. You can still see the solid "plug" of cooled lava which once shot up into the sky; although it would take a great deal of imagination to reconstruct the original crater, which has long since been worn away by water, wind and ice. Once, too, there were volcanoes in Snowdonia, and in the West country, but there is no danger now that they will erupt. They have been extinct for millions of years, and our nearest volcanoes today are in Italy and Iceland.

Since the earth began, volcanoes have appeared, erupted and then died. We know that in the past there were many more volcanoes than the 500 or so that exist today. They were also many, many times more violent. When we look at the green, and friendly countryside around us, it is hard to imagine the immense forces at work far below the surface, which have shaped the hills and fields, mountains and valleys where we live.

7 This is the strange lunar landscape left after a volcano has erupted. You can see the lava which has now cooled to become rock.

8 With the lava comes a storm of volcanic ash which rains down on the countryside. Here you can see the white volcanic ash which covered a forest in Hawaii.

1 Here you can see the birth of a volcanic island. It is called Surtsey and it is just south west of Iceland. In November 1963, a submarine volcano poured out lava and the violence of the eruption began pushing the island up out of the sea.

2 A few months later, there was a tiny island, where none had existed before, still smoking from the heat of the eruption. Islands like this quite often appear unexpectedly, and new maps have to be drawn up to include them. This especially happens in the Pacific Ocean which has a lot of volcanic islands. Very rarely, the same thing happens in reverse: a volcano will literally blow an island to pieces and it disappears under the sea.

1 Why not make a volcano out of sand? Build a cone, with sharply sloping sides.

2 Now hollow out a tunnel to reach right to the centre of the cone. Be careful not to make a landslide!

A volcano erupts

One of the world's most famous volcanoes is Mount Etna, in Sicily. It is still active and in September 1979, it erupted again, killing several tourists.

Perhaps the best-known Italian volcano is Vesuvius. On 24th August, AD 79 it erupted a huge cloud of burning gas and molten rock, destroying the surrounding countryside, and burying the beautiful Roman city of Pompei under tons of falling ash, in a few minutes. The disaster came so suddenly, that few people were able to escape in time. When archaeologists dug up the old city, they found everything as it was, on an ordinary summer morning nearly two thousand years ago - the cats and dogs, the shops, street life and even the day's bread in the oven.

◀ 3 Now using a stick, make a chimney from the point of the cone to reach your tunnel.

4 Collect some balls of crumpled newspaper and stuff them into your tunnel. Set light to them and watch your volcano smoke!

5 Your volcano will not throw up lava – but it will smoke and you may even see flames from its red-hot interior!

1 This is the river Kenai in Alaska. As it slowly winds its way it drops sand and mud, making its curves even wider.

How the land was formed

Not all the mountains were made in a distant fiery period of the earth's history. Some of our highest mountain ranges are still growing today. Centimetre by centimetre, the Alps and the Himalayas are being pushed higher and higher.

The earth's crust is broken up into huge plates. Where two of these vast plates, carrying whole continents, are scrunching together, the pressure is so great that the rock in between is crumpled up and thrust into the air.

But the story is even stranger than this. If two plates are squeezing up together at one end, a *new* crust is oozing up from under the earth at the other end

2 Here is Wyoming, in North America. Here you can actually see, by looking at the layers in the rock, how they have been pushed upwards by huge pressure.

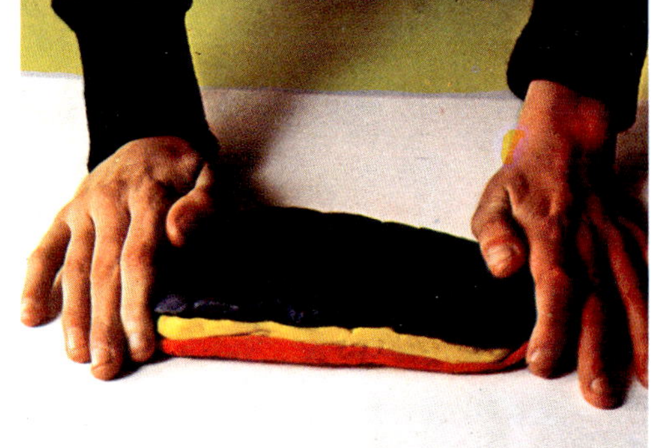

3 & 4 The earth's crust is made up of huge plates. Where these are pushed together, there are enormous stresses. Sometimes, mountains are thrust into the air by the pressure. You can try "folding" a piece of plasticine yourself. That is what happens to rock.

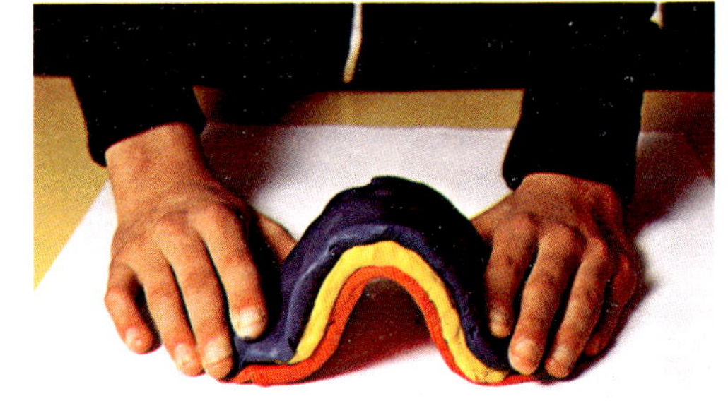

to fill the gap. This is happening today on the ocean bed, just as it has done for millions of years. But, of course, it is far too slow a process for us to actually *see* it taking place.

The face of the earth has been changed by ice and by volcanoes and by fiery pressures from deep inside. But it has also been shaped by water! Over millions of years, the seas and rivers have worn away the land; rain has poured down and carved the rocks away. Slowly, slowly, tiny bits of rock have collected together and mixed with the remains of plants and living things, to make fertile soil for green grass, trees and flowers to grow in.

7 Here in the valley of the White River in South Dakota, you can see how the water has scoured away the soil and softer rock. Only the harder rock remains.

5 You can see yourself how water could wash away soil and rock.

6 You can imitate the effect of the desert wind by blowing on some semolina or flour.

8 The wind blows the desert sand into wave-like dunes. This is Saudi Arabia and these are the red sand dunes of the Dahna Desert.

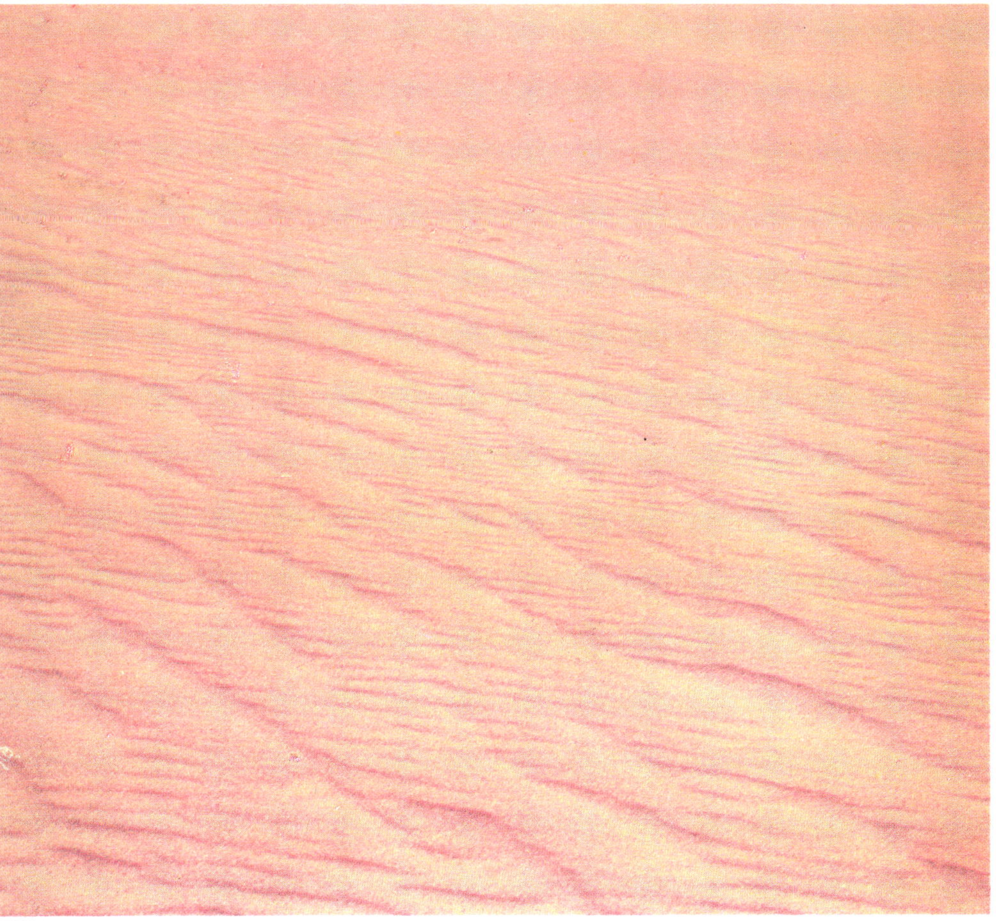

1 These fantastic archways were made by the desert wind, in a valley in Utah, North America.

2 If you damp your flour, you can imitate the strange shapes made by the wind. ▶

Sometimes a swift river will carry earth and rocks from one place and drop them hundreds of miles away when it has begun to move more slowly. If the water dries up before it can drop its load of minerals and soil, it often leaves strange and beautiful crystal patterns.

Even the wind has taken part in shaping the earth. It can carry sharp sand and dust, sculpting weird, twisted shapes as it scours away the rock.

3 This is a *geyser*, or warm spring in the Salt plains of Dancalia. When the water dries up, it leaves patterns of salt crystals.

◀ 4 You can imitate this yourself. Dissolve some salt in some water.

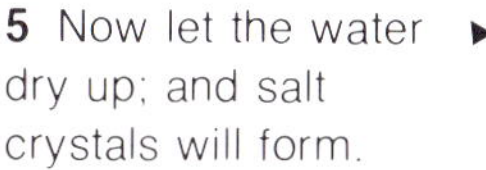

5 Now let the water dry up; and salt crystals will form. ▶

1 In the middle of the picture you can see the earth when it was hot and fiery. Slowly it cooled down and the steam from volcanoes became water which filled the seas. Once, the continents were joined together in a super-continent called *Pangaea*. Over millions of years they reached the places they are today. They are still moving; but very, very slowly indeed.

Drifting continents

If a space traveller was to look at the beautiful blue and white ball that is our world, he would probably call it "Sea" and not "Earth", as over two thirds of the planet is covered by water.

He might also notice something else. The huge continents look very much like bits of jigsaw puzzle that you could fit together. And that, we believe, is what once happened. As you know, the earth's crust is moving about very slowly in huge plates. Many millions of years ago, all the continents were joined together in one great landmass that we call *Pangaea*. England was then in the middle, near the equator and Yorkshire was a desert, like the Sahara.

Slowly, very slowly, Pangaea began to split up into the continents we now know and they drifted apart. New oceans opened up and in every country of the world, the weather changed.

Centimetre by centimetre, the continents are still moving today. England is slowly creeping southwards; although it would take many, many life-times before we could actually *see* any movement ourselves. We believe that the Red Sea is widening, and may one day become an ocean like the Atlantic; while the Mediterranean is slowly closing and so will probably not exist at all, millions of years from now.

2 This photograph, taken from an artificial satellite, shows part of the Red Sea and part of the Indian Ocean. Can you see how it looks like two pieces of gigantic jigsaw?

3 This is the Sinai Peninsula between the Mediterranean and the Indian Ocean. You can see how the land looks as if it is splitting apart.

1 This is an African lion; but it has relatives in Asia, in North America, and even in South America.

2 This is a puma, a distant relative of the lion, from the American continent, proving that animals must have at one point been able to wander from Africa to North America, probably via Europe.

Wandering animals

It is very difficult to believe that the continents are moving about. But we think it must be true. Many of the rocks on opposite sides of the oceans are identical. The layers are even the same, proving that at one time, they were joined together. We also know that in many places, the sea bed is *younger* than the continents. This means that some oceans were formed *after* the land.

But perhaps the best proof comes from the animals, birds, trees and plants. It has always sur-

3 This is a dromedary in Tunisia. Early camels once lived in North America. They also travelled to Europe and Asia.

4 This is a relation of the dromedary, the llama, which moved from North America to South America.

5 This is a wolf. Once they lived all over Europe but today they are very rare indeed although some still live in the mountains of Czechoslovakia.

6 This looks like a wolf – but it is not related at all! It is a Tasmanian Devil, from Australia, now nearly extinct.

prised scientists that animals living on different continents like Africa and South America could come from the same family. How had they crossed the Atlantic Ocean? It is much too wide for them to swim! We now guess that although by the time mammals had developed, the continents were very much as we see them today, *land bridges* must have remained between them. Fossils from all over the world tell the same story: Europe and North America must once have been joined because we have found remains of the same early ancestor of our modern horse in both places.

7 This is a European mole, living in the dark in his underground tunnel.

8 This animal is not a mole. It is a marsupial from Australia, and it has grown to look like a mole because it lives in very much the same way.

The beginning of the world

1 This is an ancient Hindu dance called the *Dance of Sita*. It is performed in a circle; and describes some scenes from the life of the great hero Rama, one of the earthly forms of the god Vishnu, and his wife Sita. We on earth are used to everything around us moving in circles, or *cycles*, and we imitate this pattern in our own lives.

2 This photograph was taken from a satellite. Even the weather systems move in spirals, while a hurricane, like this one, is a whirling circle of storm and wind.

The universe is in continual motion

As far back as we can trace, the world has been constantly changing, moving, reforming or breaking down; fast or slow, everything, everywhere is moving: nothing stays still.

In our world, many things seem to move roughly in a *circle*. Everything on our planet - stones, trees, dust and even people - is made up of tiny *atoms*. Circling round the centres of these minute particles, like satellites, are even tinier *electrons*, which are so small that we cannot even see them with the most powerful microscopes.

Our earth itself is spinning in space while the moon, our satellite, circles round us. But we are only one of nine planets that travel round the sun, making up what we call the *solar system*. Our solar system belongs to a much larger group of stars called a *galaxy*. If we look up at the night sky, we can see the rest of our galaxy and we call it the Milky Way. From our view on earth, it looks like a stream of tiny points of light. But if we could look at it from outer space, we would see that the stars in the galaxy form a tight spiral.

Years ago, people refused to believe that the earth was not the centre of the universe. They were frightened by the idea that the earth went round the sun, once a year. Today, they would be very disturbed to discover that our solar system is also travelling. We believe that our sun makes a complete journey round the centre of the galaxy about once every 225 million years. It is not surprising then, that we on earth have become used to everything going round in circles or *cycles*; we know that spring follows winter, summer follows spring and that the process will repeat itself, year in, year out.

1 If you follow the spiral in the picture, beginning from the outside, you will see how we believe the solar system began - out of a vast cloud of gas. Slowly, the sun and planets formed; but eventually, when the sun grows old, it will turn into a huge ball of fire and in the end it will probably explode.

How the earth was made

But what happened before the earth was made? How was the solar system created? Scientists believe there was once a time of immense explosions, and heat, which we on earth can hardly imagine.

All the planets in the solar system - and the sun - seem to be made of the same materials, and they are all roughly the same age: about 5,000 million years old. We now believe that the solar system was once a vast cloud of spinning gas. Slowly it shrank, forming our sun, with its nine planets - including earth - revolving around it.

Our sun is like a huge energy-producing factory. Inside, at temperatures we can only guess at, it is actually *changing* the materials from which it is made from one thing to another, in a tremendous atomic reaction, throwing out millions of degrees of heat as it does so.

But where did the materials come from to form the gas cloud that became the solar system? Perhaps they came from other old and decaying stars, which had exploded, scattering a vast stock-pile of materials all over space. In this way, the plants and animals on our earth and all the other planets began with the birth and death of stars.

2 There have been several theories about how the earth was formed. After all, no one was there to *see* it happen! Some people once believed that the planets were made from pieces torn off another sun, which cooled and began circling *our* sun.

3 Other people believed that two stars crashed together, breaking off pieces which cooled down to become the planets. But today, this is no longer thought to be true.

4 Another idea was that the planets were floating pieces of matter which were attracted by the sun – rather in the way a magnet attracts a piece of iron – and so began circling round it.
All these theories are perhaps no stranger than some of the creation myths which people have believed in ancient times. You can read some of them on the next few pages.

The creation story from the Bible

The very first chapter of the Bible, is called Genesis, and starts with the words, "In the beginning, God created heaven and earth." We do not know who wrote this - it may have been several people - but it was certainly many hundreds of years ago. Like many other ancient accounts of the birth of the world, it is written in picture-language.

The unknown author goes on to say that earth was once formless and empty. Only God moved in the darkness which covered immense waters.

Then God said, "Let there be light;" and there was light. God saw that the light was good and He divided it from the darkness. In this way, the first Day and the first Night were created.

On the second Day, God said, "Let there be heaven," and he created a broad firmament dividing the waters in two, so that some were above heaven and some below.

On the third Day, He said, "Let the waters under heaven gather together in one place and let the dry land appear also." In this way, the seas and the earth were made; and God saw that they, too, were good. Then He said, "Let the earth bring forth all green things and let fruit grow on the trees. Every plant shall bear a seed."

On the fourth Day, God said, "Let there be lights in heaven, so that Day shall be divided from Night. These lights shall show the changing seasons and the passing years;" and He made the Sun, the Moon and the stars.

On the fifth Day, He said, "Let the seas bring forth all fish and water creatures, and let birds fly in the skies; and may they flourish and multiply."

On the sixth Day, God said, "Let the earth bring forth every kind of living creature and creeping thing, and may they cover the earth with their kind." Then He said, "Let us make Men in our image, and let them rule over all the other creatures that have been made." So God made Mankind, both male and female and He blessed them. Then He looked and saw the great multitude of creatures and He saw that it was good.

On the seventh Day, God rested after His works of creation.

How the earth was born from an egg

The people of Finland have an ancient poem which describes the creation of the world and the mythical early heroes. It is called the *Kalevala*. It tells how the first living creature of all was Luonnotar, the beautiful daughter of Air. She lived alone in the heavens for thousands of years, looking down at the great empty seas until at last she grew sad and weary of the huge nothingness all around her. She came down from the heavens and swam in the water, floating where the wind and waves would take her.

Time passed, and a duck flew across the sky, searching in vain for somewhere to rest. She was so exhausted that she was about to tumble into the sea, when Luonnotar saw her and lifted her knees above the water. Thankfully, the duck rested on this strange new island and began to build herself a nest.

Soon, there were six golden eggs in the nest, and one of iron, and the duck sat on them to keep them warm. There she sat for two whole days (at that time, days were not our days, they were whole ages and generations). Luonnotar felt her knees growing warmer and warmer, and although she wanted to move, she kept still.

On the third day, she could bear it no longer and stretched her knees into the water. The eggs fell into the sea and broke.

But as the shell of the iron egg split in two, one half rose up and became the sky. The other fell back and became the earth. The yolk of the egg was the sun, and the white flew into the sky to become the moon; while the tiny pieces of broken shell became the clouds and stars.

Years passed by, and Luonnotar continued to swim in the calm and silent waters of the sea. At the end of the ninth year she rose up and began the Creation. Where her hand touched, bays and cliffs appeared. Her feet pressed the earth into mountains and deep valleys opened up before her, while her sweeping arms formed the great plains and deserts. She returned to the sea and, swimming on her back, she covered the surface with tiny islands and rocks. In this way, Finland was born; and with it, the rest of the world.

When the sun and the moon were united

From Africa comes a story about a time when sun, moon and water lived together on earth. Not a day passed but the sun or the moon went to visit their friend the water. But the sun grew discontented.

"I visit water daily; but never, never does she come to see me," he complained to his wife, the moon.

"Ask her the reason for this," advised his wife. So the sun went to see water.

"Why don't you come to visit me?" he asked.

"Because your house is not big enough," replied the water with a gentle smile. "If I were to arrive with all my relations, we would drive you out of house and home." The sun begged and pleaded and at last, water agreed to visit him on one condition: that he built a huge house, big enough for her and all her great family.

The sun returned home to tell the moon the news and straight away, he began work on the great house. Many months later when it was finished, the sun sent water an invitation and soon she arrived.

"Are you sure I can come in?" she asked. "Of course," said the sun. "Everything is ready."

So the water trickled in, together with all the thousands of creatures that lived with her: the fish came with the crocodiles and the hippos; even the tiny snails came with the newts and frogs. In a few minutes, the house was ankle-deep in water.

"Are you sure I can come in?" asked water again.

"But of course," said the sun. So the water went on flowing into the house. Soon it was up to the sun's neck, but still he kept saying that there was plenty of room. At last, the sun and moon had to climb onto the roof, while water streamed into the house. "Are you *sure* I can come in?" she asked. "Oh, yes," said the sun and moon together. The water asked no more.

Slowly she rose and rose until the land became sea and only the tops of the tall mountains were showing. The sun and moon had to leave the earth and climb into the sky to save themselves - and they have stayed there ever since.

The earth was created by Pan-Ku from an egg

A myth from South China tells the story of Pan-Ku, who was the source of every living creature.

Before the Earth was, there was Chaos, and it was shaped like an egg. In the middle of this egg Pan-Ku was created, and he lived there quietly for eighteen thousand years, without moving.

Slowly, very slowly Heaven and Earth began to separate out of Chaos, just as mud settles at the bottom of a still pond. Pure, light elements flew upwards to become Heaven, and the heavy Earth fell downwards.

Pan-Ku now began to grow very swiftly. Nine times a day he changed; at one moment he was a god in Heaven, and the next he was a god on Earth. Every day, the Heavens rose three metres higher and the Earth sank downwards by the same amount. This went on for eighteen thousand years until the Heavens reached their proper height above the Earth. In the middle, Pan-Ku grew long and wide. He was the first life and the ancestor of every one of the ten thousand different living creatures on Earth.

His body forms the surface of the Earth, the plains, valleys and cliffs. His left eye became the sun and his right eye the moon, while his head became a sacred mountain. His flowing blood became the rivers, lakes and oceans, and his long, curling hair grew as grass, trees and all the green things on the Earth.

The wise men tell us that his tears welled up and flowed as the Blue River and the Yellow River, the two great rivers of China. His breath gave birth to the wind, and we hear the echo of his voice in the thunder. Lightning darts from the pupils of his eyes and the clouds are dark and brooding when he is angry, while he shows his happiness with sunshine and blue skies.

His body marks the five points of the compass (for the Chinese have five points and not four). His arms and legs made the mountains of the East and West, North and South, while his belly is the fifth point, the Central Mountain.

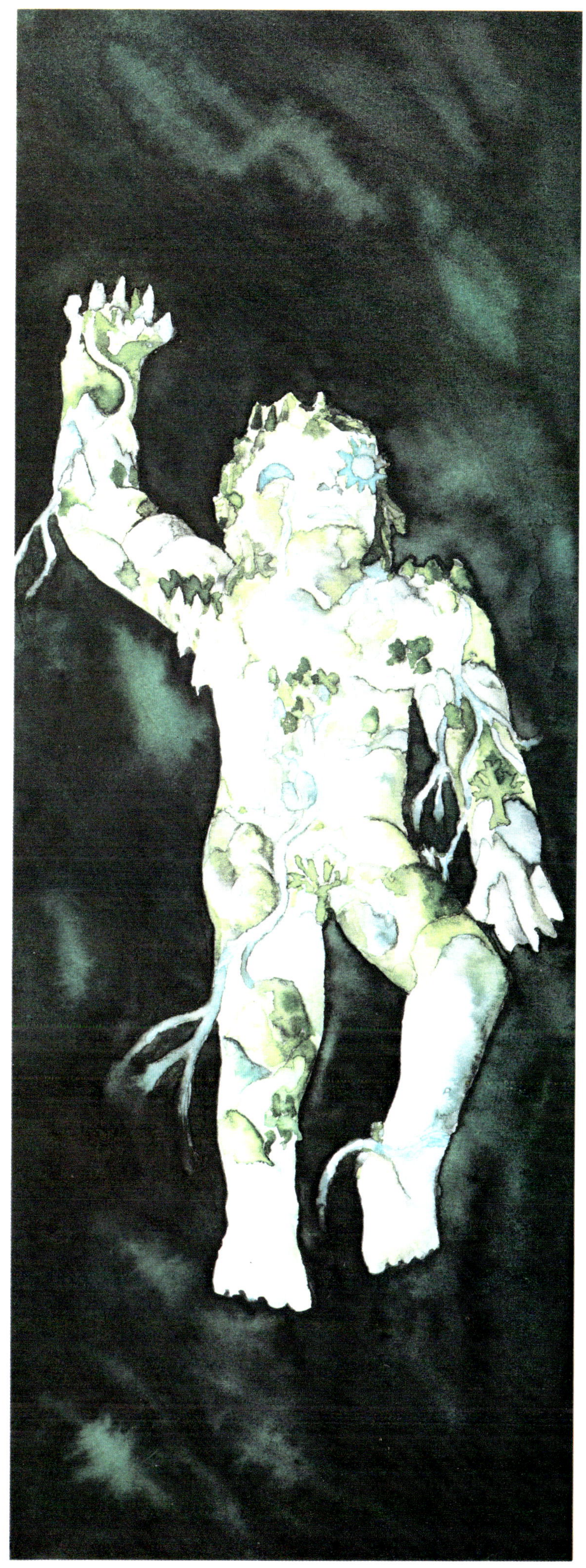

God made the earth from the bottom of the sea

The Popol Vuh is a collection of stories of the Maya Quiche Indians who lived in Central America. They tell of the creation of the world.

In the beginning, there was only the wide, empty sky and the sea. Nothing moved because there was no life on earth: no woman or child; no fruit nor flower; nothing but sky and the calm, still sea.

Above the water, glittering brightly, flew the first gods. Amongst them, hidden under green and blue feathers, were Tepeu and Gucumatz, the creators.

One evening, while the gods were gathered together meditating amongst themselves, Gucumatz spoke and said, "Let us begin a new world and create life, which will praise us and make offerings to us." All the gods agreed; and this was how, in the darkness of night, it was decided to create the first day on earth.

The dawn broke.

"Earth!" said Gucumatz. And at that moment, the new world rose up from the waters, complete and whole. In an instant, the mountains and valleys were carved from living rock, the flat plains laid bare and the earth was covered with green grass and flowers. As the high mountains rose up through the sea, the waters divided and began tumbling down the slopes as rivers and streams. Where they came to rest, they became lakes and broad, shining oceans. And cyprus forests sprang up on the mountain-sides and many rich, sweet-smelling bushes and shrubs opened their leaves to the new sun.

But the gods had not yet finished. They created then all the animals of the forests and plains, the birds and insects, the serpents and the spirits of wood, stone and field. The deer ran amongst the trees and the cattle wandered through the grass of the wide plains. The birds built nests in the newly made branches and twigs while insects hummed in the flowers.

Then the gods paused and waited for all these creatures to praise them. But they had no voices to call on the gods by name. They could only howl and hiss and roar and croak and cackle.

When the gods saw that it was impossible to make the creatures praise them, and call upon them by name, they were angry.

"This will not do," they said. "You shall live for ever in the mountains and woods, and as a punishment you shall serve as food for each other. The tiger shall eat the deer and the birds shall swallow tiny insects and worms. We will make another race of creatures to obey us and worship us."

Then the gods took clay and modelled little figures in the likeness of men. But the rains came and the figures melted into shapeless mud.

So the gods tried again. They carved little men out of wood; but although they moved and danced and spoke, they had no souls and they could not praise their creators. The gods became angry and swept them off the face of the earth in a great flood.

"We will try one last time," they said, and they pounded to flour the white and yellow maize and moulded it into figures of men. Because they were made of sacred food, they were the first true men. There were four of them, one for each corner of the earth, and the gods created four women to travel with them. These people had minds and hearts, and they understood their creation and worshipped the gods as they should.

The beginning and the end

After we had finished a meal of roast meat and baked fruit, I felt very tired; it was good to be lying on a warm rug in front of the fire. Sam and Susa were playing some kind of a game with polished pebbles. With a sudden jolt, I thought of home. "Sam," I whispered, "we've got to get back. They'll wonder where we are." Sam turned round.

"I don't want to go yet," he said. "Mur is going to show me how to make a spear-head and anyway, it's dark outside."

I panicked. "Look, Sam, we must go *now*!" He was embarrassed that I was making such a fuss. He stood up and we went to the mouth of the cave. The moon was shining and we could see the path through the fir trees that led to our time machine.

"Come on, Sam," I begged. Our modern clothes were neatly folded on a stone outside. I picked them up, whistled for Mikko and with a couple of quick backward glances, we stole off down the track. We found the time machine easily and climbed inside.

You might think that we went straight home; but we didn't. We went back to the time of the dinosaurs, to fetch Selina, our cat. And then, because we were still curious, we went back even further to before life on earth had begun, to fetch the blonde-haired doll.

Finally, Sam twisted the winder on our time clock and we shot forward into the twentieth century and our back garden. Stiffly, Sam and I climbed out of the machine. Something was very strange, and for a moment, I couldn't work out what it was.

"Sam!" I shouted. "It's still afternoon!"

Nothing had changed. Mum was still painting in the kitchen and I could see that we had taken no time at all, even though we had been gone for hours.

Then Dad put his head out of the window and shouted,

"I told you to clear up your mess; not to make another one!" Slowly, we started putting things away. Neither of us had the energy to argue. I think Dad was amazed at how quiet we were and in a while, he and Mum came out on the lawn with some iced lemon.

"I feel so *tired*," I said.

"So do I," agreed Sam. "I think I'm going to bed."

As we went indoors, I could hear Mum saying anxiously, "I do hope they're all right," and Dad said, "It's probably a touch of the sun."

If only they knew!

In this book

Summary of sections

Things to do

Stories

General Index

Index of artists

Index of plants and animals

Acknowledgements

The publishers extend their grateful thanks to copyright owners for the use of the following photographs and illustrations:

Illustrations
Gabriele Amadori 23, 33, 95, 132, 138, 139. Valentina Carpi 3, 14, 15, 113. Paolo Giorsetti 118, 119. Desideria Guicciardini 6, 8, 9, 24, 25, 49, 64, 65, 66, 67, 68, 69, 100, 101, 146. Valentino Parmiani 84, 85. Gianni Pegoraro 58, 59, 78, 79. Michele Sambin 140, 141, 142, 143, 144.

Photographs
Archivio Scala 77. Enzo Arnone 54; 55; 56; 57; 104; 105; 120; 121. Giancarlo Baghetti 87, *4*. Bartlett/Coleman 89, *3*. Marco Bellavita 39; 70; 71; 72; 73; 96, *7, 11*; 97, *17*; 115, *1, 2, 3*; 117. Alberto Borgia 26; 27. Burton/Coleman 83, *1, 2*; 103, *3*; 109, *4*. Caramelli/Mondadori 29, *6*. Paolo Carpi 90. Nino Cirani 28, *2*; 30, *1, 4*. Bruce Coleman 88. Giancarlo Costa 82, *5*; 108, *1*. Sergio Dahó 91. Dulevant 128, *2*; 129, *5*; 134, *2*; 137. Erize/Coleman 89, *6*. Fiore 17, *8*; 134, *4*. Foot/Coleman 75, *3*.Gillsater/Coleman 89, *4*. Gorro/Life/Mondadori 16, *1*; 18; 53, *4*. Havorsen/Coleman 89, *5*. Lotti/Mondadori 30, *3*. Guglielmo Mairani 22; 29, *5*; 30, *2*; 31; 48, *1, 2, 4, 5, 6*; 126. Aldo Margiocco 16, *2*; 21, *4, 5*; 34, 4; 35, *14*; 50; 80, *2*; 102; 106; 107; 110, *1*; 111, *3*; 116; 135. Mondadori Press 23. Museo della Scienza 87, *3*. NASA/UTET 133. Diane Nelson 115. Payne/Coleman 83, *4*. Pellagrini/Mondadori 122; 131, *3*. Pizzi 34, *6, 7*; 35, *8, 9, 10, 11, 13*; 82, *6*. Plage/Coleman 89, *4*. Planet News Ltd 76, *2*. Pulitzer 110, *2*. Quarishy/Coleman 83, *5*. Folco Quilici 10; 11; 13; 16, *3, 4*; 17, *6, 7*; 19; 20; 21, *2, 3*; 29, *3*; 32: 34, *5*; 40; 46; 47; 51, *2*; 53, *2, 3, 5*; 62; 63; 75, *2*; 80, *1*; 81; 86; 103, *1, 2*; 108, *2*; 109, *3*; 111, *4*; 112, 114; 123; 124; 125; 128, *1*; 129, *8*; 130, *1*; 134, *1, 3*; 136. Root/Coleman 74. Alberto Salza 12. Schranl/Jacana 83, *3*. Livia Sismondi 41; 42; 43; 95; 96, *2, 3, 4, 5, 6, 8, 9, 10*; 97, *12, 13, 14, 15, 16, 18*; 127; 128, *3, 4*; 129, *6, 7*; 130, *2*; 131, *4, 5*. Toso 17, *5*. UTET 29, *4*. Amedeo Vergani 51, *1*. Zardini/-Mondadori 34, *1, 2, 3*; 35, *12*.

The publishers would also like to thank the children of the Via Borsa Primary School, Milan; the Gemelli Primary School, Milan; the Via S. Orsola Primary School, Milan and their headmaster Maurizio Cottino; and the children from the Biblioteca Comunale di Baggio, Milan and their art adviser Renato Gostoli. Thanks are also due to the Museum of Science and Technology, Milan and to Ramzzotti Designs and Giancarlo Baghetti for permission to photograph material in their possession.

Our thanks also go to Editori Riuniti, Rome, for *Jasper, or how the wolf was outwittcd*, which was adapted from 'Tredicino' in the *Encyclopedia della favola* 1970. To Methuen Ltd for the pictures by Congo p. 76 which were taken from *The Biology of Art* by Desmond Morris, 1962. To Field Newspaper Syndicate for permission to use the cartoons on p.94 from *B.C.* by Johnny Hart. To UTET, Torino, for the illustrations of the wandering continents p. 133 which were taken from *Il Nostro Universa – La Terra* by Livio Trevisan and Ezio Tangiorgi 1976. To Memorie dell'Istituto Italiano di Idrobiologia, vol.32 Suppl., 1975, *International Symposium on Tardigrades* for the illustration on p.115 of a tardigrade. Also to Colin McNaughton for the illustrations on p.94 and p.147.